PERSONAL FINANCIAL PLANNING

D1496604

PERSONAL FINANCIAL PLANNING

Byron E. Woodman, Jr., Esquire
Stephen R. Dooley, C.P.A.
Edward S. Heald

BRICK HOUSE PUBLISHING COMPANY
Andover, Massachusetts

Library of Congress Cataloging in Publication Data

Woodman, Byron E.
 Personal financial planning.

 Includes index.
 1. Finance, Personal. I. Dooley, Stephen R.
II. Heald, Edward S.   III. Title.
HG179.W578   1987   332.024   87-13229
ISBN 0-931790-77-8

Contents

Preface

There are many ways to get advice about money—from publications, television, relatives, even golf partners or cab drivers. But someone serious about financial planning should take advantage of professional advice.

Here is where this book comes in. Making use of the latest insights into the 1986 Tax Reform Act, it gives an overview of tax planning, investing in marketable securities, tax-advantaged investments, life insurance, estate planning, and estate and trust administration.

At leisure you can examine, in convenient question-and-answer format, the comments, recommendations, and observations of the authors and contributors who prepared the book.

These professionals explain what's important and back it up with practical examples, including detailed case studies of moderate-income and high-income families.

The objective of this book is to provide you with an introduction to the topics which should be addressed when you initiate or review a program for your tax, financial and estate benefit.

Byron E. Woodman, Jr.
Stephen R. Dooley
Edward S. Heald

About the Authors

Byron E. Woodman, Jr., an attorney, is president of Woodman and Eaton, P.C., Concord, Massachusetts, a law firm concentrating in tax and estate planning, estate and trust administration, business planning, and real estate.

Stephen R. Dooley is a Certified Public Accountant with Mullen & Company, a Boston, Massachusetts, accounting firm. Mr. Dooley specializes in corporate tax planning for closely held businesses and income and estate tax planning for individuals.

Edward S. Heald is Vice President of the investment firm A.G. Edwards and Sons, Inc., which ranks among the nation's oldest and largest New York Stock Exchange members. Mr. Heald, branch manager of the Wellesley, Massachusetts, office of Edwards, specializes in tax and investment planning for businesses and professionals.

About the Contributors

William L. Eaton, Esquire, is Vice President of Woodman and Eaton, P.C. **Timothy F. Lenicheck**, Esquire, is Vice President, Financial Consulting Group, Shawmut Bank of Boston, N.A. **Terrence P. Sullivan** is President of Boston Bay Capital, Inc. **Sidney F. Greeley, Jr.**, is a Chartered Life Underwriter and Special Agent with Northwestern Mutual Life Insurance Company.

Introduction

What is personal financial planning?

In personal financial planning, one or a group of professionals review your financial estate, present and future—your assets, existing estate plan, documents, insurance policies, investments, schedule of income and expenses, employee benefits, prospective inheritances, prospective earning capacity, and any other factors—to draw up an overall financial plan for you.

They apply the laws of the state in which you live, together with the federal tax laws, to determine the tax results of the plan. They analyze your family situation and your goals and objectives. They then devise a plan to build and conserve your estate, and to pass on your property to whom, how, and when you wish.

Normally, they require that you complete a worksheet from which to develop the appropriate plan. A checklist for such a worksheet is given at the end of this introduction.

Since financial planning requires expertise in various fields, it is best done by a team. One of the team acts as coordinator. A financial planner to oversee the team may be helpful.

Who are the professionals?

An **attorney**, who generally reviews the legality of documents in the plan, and drafts estate-planning documents, such as wills, trusts, and powers of attorney.

An **accountant**, who prepares income-tax returns, and, with the attorney, reviews the estate-tax consequences of the existing and proposed plans. The accountant also prepares income projections and reviews the expected tax savings of the plan.

An **investment advisor**, who recommends general and specific investments, such as tax-deferred securities, retirement plans, IRAs, and so on.

A **life-insurance agent**, who reviews employer-provided insurance and evaluates overall insurance needs, including policy options, designation of beneficiaries, and policy ownership.

A **trust officer**, who represents the management and investment functions performed by institutional trustees, if trusts are part of the plan.

1

How do I find appropriate professionals?

If a financial planner is involved, he or she can recommend them. Otherwise, ask someone you know who has used them. If that is not practical, then a professional in one area can suggest those in other areas. Also, professional societies can identify members who specialize in financial planning.

Planning Worksheet Checklists

Date

	Husband	Wife
Name		
Residence		
Phone		
Occupation		
Business		
Address		
Phone		
Birthdate		
Birthplace		
Marriage date		
Marriage place		
Prior marriages		
Death or divorce?		
County of divorce		
Social Security no.		
Veteran serial no.		

Family Tree

Names and addresses of all family members, stating if deceased.

	Husband	Wife
Mother		
Father		
Brothers		
Sisters		
Children (include birthdate)		
Spouses of children		
Grandchildren		

Inventory of Assets, Liabilities
(current market values)

List by Ownership: Husband   Wife   Joint

Residence (describe; fair market value)
Real estate (second home; investment)
Bank accounts (type; bank name; current values)
Life insurance (face amount)
Securities (publicly traded stocks, bonds; values)
Liquid investments (money market funds; savings bonds; annuities; T bills)
Personal property (autos; antiques; jewelry; household furnishings; boats)
Tax shelters (type and amount)
Business ownership interest (description and value)
Notes receivable
Employment benefits (description and value: pensions, IRAs, profit-sharing, stock options)
Interests in trust (description and value, grantor, trustee, powers under trust)
Insurance (health, disability, homeowner)
Inheritance (from whom, amount, restrictions)
Liabilities (debts, mortgages, notes, guarantees, margin accounts, litigation)
Other
Income of household (present)
     Earned
     Investments
Expenses of household (present)
Income of household (projected average, five years)
     Earned
     Investments
Anticipated extraordinary future income
     (stock options, inheritance, retirement benefits, etc.)
Anticipated extraordinary future expenses
     (health, education, business buyout, etc.)
Safety deposit boxes (name, location, signatories)
Will (date, location of original)
Trust (date, location of original)
Power of attorney (date, person given, nature of power)
Financial advisors (names, addresses, phone numbers)
     Accountant, Attorney, Investment advisors, Trust officers,
     Insurance agents, and Financial planners
Additional comments

Tax Planning

Introduction

People used to throw rocks at tax collectors in ancient times. That kind of tax planning is not very useful these days. But when you have worked hard to earn a good income, you should do everything you can to preserve it.

Are you taking advantage of the tax laws which can lessen the tax bite? How can an accountant save you money and help you plan your finances?

The Tax Reform Act of 1986 is the most sweeping federal tax legislation since 1954. The dramatic lowering of marginal tax rates will require all taxpayers to reorient the way they think about taxes. Basic knowledge of some provisions of the new law could result in significant tax savings for you and your family.

Where do I start?

First let us review the *terminology* and the *concept* of the individual tax structure. The individual tax is a progressive tax based on your taxable income, which is your gross income less deductions and exemptions. Your tax burden increases as your taxable income increases.

You will need to know how much you will benefit from a deduction or from excluding income. This incremental benefit is based on a *marginal tax bracket.* That's the tax rate applied to your final dollar of income. The effective top rate will be 38.5% for 1987 and 28% for tax years thereafter. For 1988 and later years there could be a 5% surtax, resulting in a top bracket rate of 33%.

Tax *credits* reduce taxes dollar for dollar and, therefore, should not be confused with deductions, which only reduce the income subject to tax. The actual dollar benefit of a tax *deduction* depends on your marginal tax bracket. For example, if you are in a 38% marginal tax bracket, a $100 tax deduction will save you $38 in taxes.

How does this translate into tax savings?

You can save on taxes in a number of ways. One is by *deferring income.* For example, you might buy Certificates of Deposit that mature after year end and pay interest on maturity.

Another is by *accelerating deductions.* You might prepay state tax liabilities, for example, on December 31, thus incurring a deduction this year for an amount that otherwise would not have to be paid until next year.

A third is by *excluding income,* for example, investing in tax-exempt bonds.

6

A fourth is by *sheltering income*. This is done by investing in real estate or other investments that provide tax deductions today and postpone income.

What effect has the 1986 tax law had on income-tax deductions?

The Tax Reform Act of 1986 has reduced the benefit of many deductions. Miscellaneous deductions such as casualty losses, unreimbursed employee travel and transportation costs, outside salesmen's expenses not directly reimbursed, business publications, and fees for investment and tax advice are now deductible only above 2% of adjusted gross income.

Medical expenses in 1987 and beyond are deductible only if they exceed 7.5% of adjusted gross income. Sales taxes are no longer deductible. There have also been many changes to interest expense. Interest on consumer loans such as credit cards, car loans, or interest charged by the IRS for underpayment of taxes is no longer fully deductible.

Interest is deductible on loans or mortgages used to finance a principal residence or a second home, but only on loan amounts which do not exceed the purchase price of the home plus the cost of improvements.

However, interest is deductible on home loans up to the fair market value of the property if the loan is used to finance education or medical expenses.

How much money should I be earning before it makes sense to hire an accountant to help me plan my taxes?

Generally, a family should consider hiring an accountant when their annual gross income approaches $50,000. This is just a rough guideline because income potential is also important.

For example, an individual could have a relatively small cash income but could have significant potential tax liability because of restricted stock received as compensation. A restricted stock is one that is subject to forfeiture. This type of stock presents enormous tax planning opportunities.

The complexity of the return is also a factor. Some taxpayers will say that they have a relatively simple return even though, for example, the W-2 amount could be $100,000 a year. They would want to use the services of an accountant for more than just preparing a return.

Alternative Minimum Tax

How will the alternative minimum tax affect me?

The alternative minimum tax (AMT) may have some unexpected applications that could upset your tax planning. Congress was concerned that certain taxpayers with significant deductions, such as net losses from passive activities and tax-exempt interest on non-governmental bonds, were not paying their fair share of taxes. As a result, the alternative minimum tax was devised.

If you have a significant tax benefit from the above, and other so-called "preference items," then you must make certain adjustments and recompute your taxable income in order to pay what Congress believes to be a fair minimum tax for your total income. You must compute both your regular income tax and the alternative minimum tax and pay the higher figure.

How is the alternative minimum tax computed?

After you have computed your taxable income under the regular method, you add back various deductions known as "preference items" to compute the alternative minimum tax. Several of the preference items relate to special types of deductions and income exclusion items.

After adding back the preference items, you have what is termed the "alternative minimum taxable income." On a joint return, $40,000 is then subtracted from the alternative minimum taxable income ($30,000 if you're single). The result is taxed at a flat 21% rate.

Should I be concerned only about the dollar amount of a preference item?

The dollar amount of a preference item does not trigger the alternative minimum tax, but rather the percentage of the preference item in relation to your taxable income. Some taxpayers could have a large number of preference items but not pay the alternative minimum tax because their regular tax is already very high.

By way of example, if you plan to reduce your taxable income by passive losses, and if you also have a large amount of untaxed appreciation on allowable charitable contributions in the same year, the alternative minimum tax might very well be higher than your regular tax.

If your alternative minimum tax is higher, you may have lost the benefit of some deductions which do not affect the alternative minimum tax, such as the deduction for state income taxes.

8

You must compute the point at which your regular tax equals your projected alternative minimum tax and plan your investments accordingly. In case you're going to ask, it's not a simple process.

Does an installment sale affect the calculation of the alternative minimum tax?

Yes. You must report the entire amount of your gain in the year of the sale for purposes of the alternative minimum tax.

Is the impact of the alternative minimum tax always negative?

Not really. This cloud has a silver lining. Since the new alternative minimum tax has a 21% rate and you may be in the 33% tax bracket, it could be a good time to accelerate income, by taking an advance on future salary, for example.

In summary, be aware that the alternative minimum tax exists and how it could affect your tax planning. Avoid losing tax benefits from deductions because of the unexpected impact of the alternative minimum tax.

Education

If I borrow to finance my child's education, will the interest on the loan be tax deductible?

Educational loans are considered to be consumer loans. For the 1987 tax year, transition rules apply. Without a specific exemption, 65% of your interest deductions are allowable in 1987, 40% in 1988, 20% in 1989 and 10% in 1990. All consumer-loan interest deductions are eliminated in years after that.

There is an exception to this rule which should not be overlooked. Generally, interest on mortgages and loans used to finance purchases of principal residences and second homes can be deducted only on the amount of the loan equal to (or less than) the purchase price of the home, plus improvements made to it.

However, the interest on such loans used for financing education is fully deductible to the extent that the amount of the loan is equal to the fair market value of the home.

Furthermore, any transfer for educational purposes will not be subject to a gift tax or the generation-skipping transfer tax. All this is in addition to the $10,000 annual gift exclusion and the $600,000 unified credit.

Can I put money in a bank account or stocks for my children and report the income or dividends on their tax returns?

Yes you may, but under the new tax law this might not be a good idea if they are younger than fourteen. A child under age fourteen pays income tax at the custodial parent's marginal rate on unearned income in excess of $1,000. This is the so-called "kiddie tax."

Can I sell stock to my children for some nominal amount and let them sell it to pay for their own education?

To constitute a true sale, such a transaction must be for fair market value. Otherwise, the IRS might view the transaction as part sale and part gift, which could result in income and gift tax consequences for you.

Second, if the stock were given to the children outright and if the children immediately sold the stock, you could still be taxed on the entire capital gain. The IRS could argue that the only purpose was to transfer your income to your children. However, if the children held the stock and sold it at a later time, the gain would be taxable on their returns.

In what tax-deferred ways *can* I pay for my children's education?

Some of the traditional ways of planning for education, such as shifting income to children and reversionary trusts, for example, no longer have the tax advantages they once did. Thus, parents must look elsewhere.

One option is to buy tax-exempt zero-coupon bonds, which defer their income payout until a maturity date, ideally after the child reaches age fourteen.

Tax-deferred annuities, marketed by insurance companies and by some college and universities, are another alternative. They defer income until a set date, and then begin paying out a fixed income to either the child or the educational institution. These annuities will escape current income tax, but may be penalized if withdrawn before maturity.

The use of single-premium life-insurance contracts presents another opportunity. The build-up of the cash surrender value of the policy provides funds from which to borrow; however, note that interest on such loans is not fully deductible.

Are there any special arrangements I can make with the college my children will attend?

It varies from institution to institution, but some colleges provide prepayment plans. A parent invests funds in advance with the college, and tuition is then charged at substantially lower rates when the child enrolls.

Some institutions have submitted their plans to the IRS with the hope that the interest earned on amounts deposited will be tax-exempt, which would make such plans all the more attractive.

Charitable lead trusts and charitable remainder trusts provide a university with a source of income, and provide the donor with an income-tax deduction. Such giving indirectly helps the institution keep down the cost of tuition and room and board.

Are grants and scholarships available?

Grants and scholarships vary from state to state and locality to locality, but the federal government still provides assistance for education. Aid in the form of Pell Grants and Supplemental Educational Opportunity Grants (SEOGs) are available to certain qualified students. Loans may also be obtained from the Federal Education Department and the Health and Human Resources Department.

Colleges and universities also offer aid and loan programs, and students should explore aid and loans from their parent's employers, from local fraternal organizations, or from private foundations.

Not all students are eligible for the same amount of financial aid. A student's needs and academic achievement are the most important factors. Parents are required to disclose information about their own financial condition, and are expected to assist a child with educational needs.

How does a student qualify without parental contributions?

An individual could qualify as an independent student in order to be eligible for financial aid. A person should meet one of the following requirements: older than twenty-four, a veteran of the United States Armed Forces, an orphan, a single undergraduate with no dependents, not claimed as a dependent on a parental tax return, no legal dependents other than a spouse, or a married graduate student not claimed as a dependent.

Real Estate

I just bought a new house. I expect to sell my old house for a price that will net me about $50,000 as a capital gain. What is my tax return going to look like?

You can defer the tax on the capital gain if the purchase price of your new home equals or exceeds the selling price of your former home, regardless of what you originally paid for the old home. The new purchase must take place within 24 months before or after the sale of your old house.

How long can I defer the capital gain?

Until the time, if ever, you buy a *less* expensive house or no longer own a residence. When you are 55 or older, you will also be able to use the one-time exclusion of $125,000 to avoid paying some of the capital gains.

By the way, the 1986 Tax Reform Act eliminated the beneficial tax rate previously given to long-term capital gains. Capital gains are now all taxed at the same rate. However, long-term capital gains can still be offset against long-term capital losses.

Will the fact that my home mortgage is paid off affect my ability to deduct the interest for a $20,000 home-improvement loan?

No. You may borrow and deduct the interest for a loan equal to the purchase price of your home plus the $20,000.

Will I be able to deduct property rental losses in 1987?

If you actively manage a rental unit and your adjusted gross income is $100,000 or less, you will be able to deduct up to a $25,000 rental loss on your 1987 tax return. However, if your adjusted gross income is more than $100,000, then the $25,000 loss limitation is reduced by $1 for every $2 your adjusted gross income exceeds $100,000. For example, if your adjusted gross income is $140,000, the $25,000 loss limitation would be reduced to $5,000.

What if I don't manage my rental property?

If you do not actively manage the rental unit, then the $25,000 loss limitation does not apply, but the phase-in rule will apply. Under this special phase-in rule, you will be able to deduct 65% of the disallowable portion of the loss in 1987, 40% in 1988, 20% in 1989, 10% in 1990, and none in years thereafter. Any non-deductible rental losses could be carried over to future years to offset net income from the rental or sale of this property.

Will I be able to deduct losses claimed on vacation property that I rent out?

If the property is actively managed by you, it is subject to the rules described above. However, if the property is your seasonal home and you do not rent it, you may deduct the interest and taxes paid on it.

In 1987, I sold some rental property, taking the proceeds in quarterly installments. May I use the installment method of reporting the sale?

Yes. However, there are rules effective in 1987 you must follow. Under the old law, you only recognized a pro rata share of the gain as you received each cash payment. Now, when the sale price exceeds $150,000, you may recognize a portion of the gain not only on the cash you receive but also on a portion of your outstanding indebtedness for the year.

This situation may occur if you have a high ratio of business debt compared to your total assets. This ratio will be applied to your installment receivable and the result will be considered a cash payment received by you. Your gross profit percentage realized on the investment sale will then be applied to the cash payment.

Taxes on Investments

Is interest expense on investments affected by the phasing out of interest deductions on consumer debt?

No. The 1986 tax law has a separate set of rules applicable to investment interest expense. Under the old law, such interest was deductible to the extent that investment income exceeded investment expenses, plus a $10,000 exemption.

The exemption has been eliminated, and investment income in this calculation cannot include income from passive activity (such as rental income).

Will this change be phased in?

Yes, on the same schedule as consumer loan interest. Of the $10,000 exemption, 65% will be allowed in 1987, 40% in 1988, 20% in 1989, 10% in 1990, and none thereafter.

You should be careful in calculating net investment income during this phase-in period, because you must deduct any passive-activity losses you are otherwise allowed to take during the phase-in period for reducing those deductions.

Does this mean that I must reduce my investment income by the amount of a rental-loss deduction?

Not exactly. You may take a rental-loss deduction from your income tax without reducing your investment income. However, any rental losses *not* deducted from your taxable income must be deducted from your investment income.

May I use the installment method for sales of a portfolio of publicly traded stocks and bonds?

No. If your stocks and bonds are publicly traded, the use of the installment method of selling is, for tax purposes, denied completely.

How are long-term capital gains affected by the 1986 tax law?

The maximum tax rate for long-term capital gains is increased from an effective 20% in 1986, to 28% in 1987, and 33% in 1988 and beyond.

15

How did you arrive at 20% for 1986?

In 1986 only 40% of long-term capital gains was taxable, and the maximum tax rate was 50%. Multiplying one by the other gives 20% of the total gain as being taxable. Beginning in 1988, 100% of long-term capital gains are taxable, at the rates above, until they reach the maximum ordinary tax rate of 33%.

Does the same apply to short-term capital gains?

Yes and no. In 1987 short-term capital gains may be taxed up to the maximum ordinary tax rate of 38.5%. However, in 1988 both short and long-term gains will be taxed at the maximum ordinary rate of 33%.

Must I still reduce a long-term capital loss carryover by 50% in applying it against a capital gain?

No. The 1986 tax law allows deduction of long-term capital losses dollar for dollar against gains. However, the maximum capital-loss deduction against ordinary income remains at $3,000.

How will the tax laws affect S corporations?

S corporations are like chameleons. Legally they are corporations, but they are treated much like partnerships from a tax point of view. With some exceptions, all income and loss flows directly to the shareholders for declaration on their personal tax returns.

This results in only one layer of taxation, although a double tax may be imposed on collection of accounts receivable and disposition of undervalued assets existing at the time a company is converted to an S corporation.

What about tax rates and accounting methods?

Individual tax rates will be lower than corporate rates by the time the 1986 tax law is fully phased in. Also, an S corporation may benefit from using a cash-basis accounting method rather than the accrual method. The cash method may allow more flexibility in tax planning and assist a growing company in capital formation, because it is not required to pay taxes on billings not yet collected.

Tax Shelters

What is a passive income activity?

A "passive income activity" includes any business in which the taxpayer is not involved on a "regular, continuous and substantial basis throughout the year." The tax law specifies that limited-partnership interests and rental property will be treated as passive income activities, regardless of whether or not the taxpayer materially participates in their management.

What does the tax law say about passive income activity?

You cannot deduct passive-investment losses from salary, interest, dividends, capital gains and other active business income. Losses from passive activities are deductible only from income from other passive activities.

The passive loss rule takes effect in 1987, and will be phased in over five years at the same rate as the limitations on consumer interest deductions: 65% of the losses allowable in 1987, 40% in 1988, 20% in 1989, 10% in 1990, and none thereafter.

However, any losses not deducted may be carried forward indefinitely, and used to offset passive activity income. This means that you should consider trying to generate as much passive income as possible to use any passive losses you may have.

What else should we know about passive income activity?

Unusable passive losses may be carried forward indefinitely and applied against passive income in later years. Passive losses will be allowed before passive activity tax credits. Passive tax credits may also be carried forward indefinitely.

Passive tax credits are to be aggregated with other tax credits, and are subject to the general limitations on tax credits. For instance, only 75% of the tax liability over $25,000 may be offset by credits.

What happens if a passive activity is sold?

When the taxpayer sells the entire interest in a passive activity, any carryover losses may be fully deductible. However, tax credits may still be allowable, but only to the extent of a tax liability on passive income.

The 1986 tax law specifies that a taxpayer may not deduct suspended losses or credits upon disposition of less than an entire interest in a passive activity.

Moreover, a transfer that merely changes the form of ownership will not qualify as a disposition allowing such deductions.

How does this apply to rental property income?

Rental activities are considered passive activities regardless of whether or not the taxpayer materially participates in the activity. However, as mentioned earlier, depending on the taxpayer's gross income and active participation in managing a real-estate investment, up to $25,000 of losses and credits from the activity may be used to offset non-passive income.

"Active participation" in a rental activity does not require "regular, continuous and substantial" involvement in the business, but it does require significant and bona fide participation. Bona fide participation includes participating in management decisions regarding rental rates and terms, and arranging for maintenance and repairs.

However, regardless of the taxpayer's level of participation, he will not be treated as "actively participating" if he owns less than 10% of the rental activity.

Investments

Introduction

According to the wag Kin Hubbard, the safest way to double your money is to fold it over once and put it in your pocket. No investment advice, however, is universal; designing an investment program is a highly individual matter.

Each person's strategy will be different, depending on his particular needs and priorities. But there are certain issues everyone should consider in designing an investment program to meet his goals.

An investment program is essential. Over the past fifteen years, the consumer price index has nearly tripled. Unless an individual's assets on an after-tax basis also tripled, that individual lost ground. What should that individual have invested in? Historically, common stocks, real estate, and other equity-related investments have produced returns in excess of inflation.

How much money should be devoted to investments?

In addition to day-to-day living expenses, three major expenses take precedence over investments. First, you have to provide for your residence. Second, you should have a cash reserve readily available to meet fluctuations in your cash needs. Third, you must protect yourself from financial catastrophe with insurance.

You should probably have health insurance, including some form of coverage for long-term care as well as acute care. Disability insurance will provide continuation of your salary if you are incapacitated, and life insurance will provide an instant estate in the event of your premature death. Finally, liability insurance can protect you from financial loss due to legal action.

How you use every dollar beyond those spent on these basic needs is an investment decision, whether you think of it that way or not.

How much cash reserve should an investor have?

A very general rule of thumb is that you should keep the equivalent of six months take-home pay in a cash reserve account, where it is readily available for unexpected needs. There are a number of factors you should consider in deciding on the right amount for your own situation; for example, the terms of your disability income insurance, the amount of your other assets, and the security of your employment. Your cash reserve should be tailored to your needs and lifestyle rather than to an absolute or fixed formula.

20

Since keeping cash under the mattress has gone out of style, where should I keep my cash reserve?

A money-market account at a bank, a money-market mutual fund with check-writing privileges, six-month bank certificates of deposit (CDs), or U.S. Treasury bills which can be readily converted to cash. One advantage of treasury bills over the others is that the interest earned is exempt from state and local taxes.

What homework should I do before embarking on an investment program?

First, have a clear idea of what you want your money to do. Without this focus, you run the risk of having a conglomeration of investments with no direction.

Second, decide on a time frame during which the benefits are needed: for example, college education, family financial support, retirement income.

Third, write out a complete financial inventory, including all assets and income.

Fourth, be willing to speak frankly to an investment professional about personal biases, family situation, employment and business future, and other concerns.

How should I begin an investment program?

Common sense dictates that you should not put all your money into any one investment. Diversification over three to five different securities may be a good starting point if you have a relatively small amount to invest.

If your investment program is modest in size, you should consider mutual funds, which offer broad diversification and can be purchased for as little as $50.

As the amount of assets you have to invest increases, the degree of diversification should increase also. You should also expect to be spending more on investment advice as the account grows.

If you plan to invest substantial assets, you may want to have a privately managed individual account. Some investment advisors do accept accounts as small as $10,000, but most require a minimum of $100,000 to $250,000.

How should I approach deciding what to invest in?

The many investment opportunities can be confusing. They include everything from relatively secure investments that are liquid (easily cashed in) such as bank accounts and treasury bills on the one hand, to mutual funds, to specialized investments such as options, limited partnerships and venture capital.

What you should do first before making an investment is figure out what you want your money to do for you. You have to answer some of these questions: Do you want income, or is growth more important? How much risk are you willing to assume in aiming for higher returns? Do you need to reduce taxes? How important is the liquidity of an investment? Once you have analyzed your own needs in these terms you can put together a program to meet those needs.

Realize, however, that an investment program is dynamic—as your needs or circumstances change, your program may need to change as well. Therefore, you are not making one-time decisions, but rather are continually fine-tuning the decisions made to reflect your particular situation.

Bonds

Government and municipal bonds are supposed to be relatively safe investments. What is the risk, if any?

There is an element of market risk to all bonds. The market price of any bond, for example a long-term bond with a maturity date of ten years or more, will fluctuate with changes in interest rates. If rates go up, prices will decline, and vice versa. Thus, if you have to sell a bond prior to its maturity, you may receive more or less than you originally invested, depending on changes in interest rates.

Can I have the interest income from Treasury bills or other government bonds reinvested?

Not with individual bonds, but you do have three other alternatives. First, "zero-coupon bonds" do not provide current interest payments, but provide all the return upon maturity. For example, a zero-coupon bond bought today for $500 pays out $1,000 when it matures in eight years. That would equal interest of about 9% per year.

Second, investments called "unit trusts" allow reinvestment of the interest earned. Unit trusts offer a diversified selection of tax-exempt or other bonds. You can also choose interest payments made monthly, quarterly or semi-annually. Initial investments are as low as $1,000.

Last, certain mutual funds invest exclusively in bonds, some only U.S. government or agency bonds, some only corporate, some only tax-exempt, and some only in tax exempts of a particular state. These funds will reinvest the interest.

Are minimum investments required for U.S. Government bonds?

Yes. The minimums vary with the issuer of the bond, but the range is $1,000, $5,000, and $10,000 per bond.

Are all U.S. Government bonds exempt from state and local taxes?

No. All direct obligations of the U.S. treasury, like Treasury bills, bonds, and notes, are tax-exempt locally. In addition, certain agencies of the government,

23

such as the Federal Farm Credit Bank and the Federal Home Loan Bank, also issue bonds with interest exempt from local taxation. But not all government agency bonds are locally exempt.

Do municipal bonds yield interest that is tax exempt?

Municipal bonds are issued by state or local governments or their agencies. The interest they pay is exempt from federal taxes and, in many cases, from state and local taxes as well. Historically, they are second only to U.S. government bonds in safety. The minimum investment is normally $5,000 in any one issue.

What about other kinds of bonds?

Under the 1986 tax law, income from tax-exempt bonds issued to finance "private-purpose" facilities such as sports stadiums or industrial buildings may be subject to the alternative minimum tax. However, the size of investment required for this type of bond is so large, it is not of concern to the vast majority of the investing public.

Is there any way to minimize the market risk with bonds?

You can somewhat reduce the risk of price fluctuations by investing only in bonds which mature in two to four years. Since they mature in such a short period, the market risk is minimal.

Annuities

Are annuities safe investments?

You may want to consider purchasing what's called a single-premium tax-deferred annuity contract or a single-payment investment life contract. They are, in effect, certificates of deposit issued by an insurance company. The principal is guaranteed against loss by the assets of the insurance company, and the interest rate is comparable to other investments.

Since the guarantee of principal is backed only by the insurance company's assets, it is important to select a financially sound and well established company. The significant attraction to the fixed-rate annuity or life contract is that the interest earned is compounded with no current tax liability.

Is a tax-deferred annuity contract the proverbial free lunch, or will I have to pay income taxes on the interest some day?

Sorry, no free lunch. You will have to pay tax on the accumulated interest at some point.

If you elect to take a monthly annuity payment when you retire, the part of each payment classified as interest earned will be treated as taxable income. The advantage here is that no tax liability occurs until you choose it. Because of this feature, you can choose to take the income at a time when you are in a lower tax bracket, if that happens.

If you decide to withdraw part of the value of the contract, you will be taxed on it as interest income earned. Only after you have taken out all of the interest can you then take out non-taxable principal.

The 1986 tax law imposes a premature withdrawal penalty on an annuity contract if such withdrawal occurs prior to age fifty-nine and one half. This penalty is 10% of the amount of money withdrawn, and is added to any other tax on the withdrawal.

Clearly the IRS and Congress are stressing the use of annuity contracts as a retirement supplement, and have imposed penalties on other uses.

Stocks

In times of high inflation, will the yield from government or municipal bonds and fixed annuities be high enough to maintain the value of the investment?

There is a big difference between maintaining the dollar value of assets and maintaining the purchasing power of those assets. The types of investments discussed so far are designed primarily to return the original dollar investment intact. However, the buying power of those assets may be severely decreased by inflation.

Are there investments which do a better job of protecting purchasing power against inflation?

In order to realize a gain in purchasing power from an investment, you must be willing to own assets directly, such as a share of a business, or real estate, or a natural resource. This means accepting a higher level of risk. In return, you have the opportunity to exceed the inflation rate and make real gains in buying power.

If common stock is one type of investment with potential to keep pace with inflation, how does an investor know if a particular stock is a "good deal"?

Make sure the character of the stock will meet your needs. If you want current income, you should not buy a non-dividend-paying, high-technology stock which is expected to produce only growth. On the other hand, if you're looking for growth, and you are presented with a stock whose main attraction is its yield, you can see that the match between needs and opportunity may not be there.

Secondly, investigate the company behind the stock thoroughly. Get to know the industry, and the standing of the company in the industry. You should look into the quality and appeal of the products or services offered, and the capabilities of the management behind the company. This is called *fundamental analysis.*

Then you may want to use *technical analysis* to determine if the stock price today represents fair value in the context of prior stock price history and future prospects.

How does a person go about technical analysis of a stock?

Technical analysis is essentially the study of the history of two key components of a stock: previous price action and the volume of shares traded at these previous prices. Under pure technical analysis, very little attention is given to what the company does or what its financial condition is. The theory is that future prices can be determined entirely by a study of prior price action.

An individual investor should probably use a combination of fundamental and technical analysis. For example, fundamental analysis can help you determine whether a particular company's stock is worth owning, while technical analysis can assist you in determining whether this is the appropriate time to buy that stock.

What are some sources for background on a company and its prior stock history?

There are a variety of such sources to investigate. First, there are published research services such as Standard and Poor's Reports and The Value Line Investment Survey.

Second, most of the larger securities brokerage firms have research departments which produce in-depth analyses. There are also independent research organizations like Argus Research or Babson's Reports.

In addition, information is made available by the companies themselves in their annual and quarterly reports.

Finally, you may be able to get useful background on a company from publications such as Fortune, Business Week, Forbes and the like.

Are current yield versus future growth the only two issues to consider in buying stock, or are there other tradeoffs?

The opportunity a stock offers will fit into one of five general categories. First is income. Second is reasonable income with potential for modest growth in both income and price. Third is high-quality growth. Fourth is what's known as "businessman's risk," or more aggressive growth. Fifth are special situations where a significant change is expected within the company which could affect its future tremendously. There are benefits to each of these different types of opportunities.

What is an "income" stock?

An "income-stock" company distributes the majority of its earnings in dividends to its shareholders. Not much income is kept for reinvestment by the corporation itself. As an example, most utility companies fall into this category. Therefore, an investor will receive the bulk of the return from an investment as current income.

How does a "reasonable income" stock differ from an "income" stock?

A stock that is in the reasonable income category may not have as high a current income as the first category, but will probably offer greater potential for future increases in income. In addition, the company may offer better growth opportunity in the form of appreciation in value of the stock itself. For example, some insurance companies and companies involved in telecommunications seem to offer both reasonable dividends and attractive prospects for increasing dividends and growth.

How about "high-quality growth"?

The benefits to the investor of high-quality growth stock come mostly from increasing prices and capital growth, as opposed to dividend income. Obviously, this type of return is less certain, but the hope is that the results will exceed an income-oriented investment. The most commonly used illustration of high-quality growth is IBM.

What is "businessman's risk"?

The stock category called "businessman's risk" is labeled that for a good reason. Generally speaking, a company in this category will be smaller, younger or in a stage of rapid growth. Such a company is not yet firmly established.

There can be significant risk associated with investments in this category, but at the same time they may also offer substantial economic rewards, in the form of price appreciation. An example of this type would be a new company involved in making and selling computer hardware or software.

What are "special situations"?

Special situations involve companies that may be undergoing an unusual change. This could be new management, a new product, or some change in the industry. In any case, the change is expected to increase the earnings of the company substantially.

A special situation can occur in companies that fit into one of the other four categories. As a good illustration, think of the company that first developed the Crock-Pot. That company had been surviving with modest sales for many years as a manufacturer of can openers.

When the crock-pot was developed and became a virtual household necessity, their sales and earnings increased phenomenally and so did their stock price. The rebound of Chrysler is another illustration of the special-situation investment.

Mutual Funds

What is a mutual fund?

A mutual fund simply represents the pooling of assets by individuals with a common objective, to obtain the benefits of diversification and professional management which otherwise would not be available to them.

Mutual funds can invest in any of the possibilities just discussed. An individual fund will focus on a particular type of investment, or have a particular objective that guides its investment decisions.

What do "load" and "no-load" mean, as applied to mutual funds?

When you buy a load fund, a sales charge is included in the purchase price. Such funds are generally sold through securities firms. No-load funds do not include a sales charge at the time of investment, and are generally sold to the public directly by the fund, often through the mail. Some no-load funds are sold through securities firms, but they usually include a higher annual expense fee or an early withdrawal fee for a few years.

The presence or absence of a sales charge indicates nothing about performance. Performance is affected only by the judgement of the people making the investment decisions. Therefore, you should investigate the background and expertise of the fund management before you invest.

In theory, a broker offering a load fund has done that investigation, and is compensated for the investigation by the load or sales charge.

Portfolio Management

Doesn't stock analysis take a great deal of time?

Yes, it does. One important question to ask yourself when you're considering an investment program is this: How actively involved do I want to be in the day-to-day management of my money?

If the prospect of doing what we have just previously discussed seems overwhelming to you, or you do not have the time due to business, professional or personal interests, then you should consider enlisting the aid of professional money managers, people who do nothing other than analyze and manage investments on a full-time basis.

Can a securities broker manage my stock portfolio?

A full-service broker can manage your stocks, if you would like third-party opinions or access to information that may not be easily available to you, or you want someone to provide personal attention to your account. But you should bear in mind that a broker is not a pure analyst or money manager.

A broker may be able to stimulate your thinking about various opportunities as they arise. But a broker doesn't get paid to manage assets; he is paid on the basis of transactions made.

Where do discount brokers fit in?

A discount broker provides a "transaction-only" service, and charges commissions below full-service brokers. In return for the lower commission, discount brokers seldom offer any advice or guidance, may not be willing to accept securities that require legal documents, may not offer a full range of products, and do not necessarily provide personalized investor service.

It is important for the investor to weigh the worth of these additional services against the commission savings that can be realized. If you are an investor who makes all the decisions without needing outside input, then a discount broker may be all that you need.

Where else can I look for investment management?

An investment advisor's responsibility is to recommend investments appropriate for an individual's account, to monitor those investments, and to make changes when justified. You may also want an investment advisor to manage a specific portion of your assets for a particular purpose such as retirement or college education expenses.

A third category of professional assistance is a personal financial advisor who can help you formulate your goals and take the broadest view of your financial planning.

A true advisor should not have a vested interest in any particular recommendation. He or she is paid a fee, and is paid regardless of whether a transaction occurs or not. The job of the advisor is to provide unbiased professional management for an investor's account. The purchase and sale of stock is done through a securities broker.

What are some of the qualities I should look for in choosing an investment manager?

Interview a variety of professionals, including stock brokers, financial planners, and investment advisors. Select one or a combination who will listen to you and understand what you want; who has sufficient knowledge of all investment alternatives; who is able to outline advantages and disadvantages of various courses of action; and who has a perspective on the merits of a variety of investments, so as to select those which are most appropriate to your needs.

Finally, such a professional must perform periodic check-ups on the success of the investments made. He or she must be willing ruthlessly to houseclean those that do not provide the anticipated benefits.

Such a person is very valuable to you, and is well worth the search on your part.

Retirement Benefits

Has the 1986 tax law made any changes in the area of retirement benefits and pension plans?

Yes. A provision of the new law imposes a 15% excise tax when an individual dies with a so-called "excessive accumulation" or makes an "execessive-accumulation" withdrawal during lifetime.

"Excessive accumulation" is an aggregate interest in a retirement plan which exceeds an annual annuity of $112,500. The $112,500 will be indexed for inflation after 1987, and in some instances will rise to $150,000.

Are individual retirement accounts (IRAs) affected by the tax law?

You bet. Under prior law, all taxpayers with wages could make a contribution to an IRA equal to earned income or $2,000, whichever was lesser. In addition, a working couple with only one wage earner could contribute up to $2,250 to a spousal IRA.

Now, if a married couple's adjusted gross income is $50,000 or more, and one of them is covered by a retirement plan, they will be denied an IRA contribution deduction.

The deduction will be phased out pro rata for adjusted gross incomes between $40,000 and $50,000.

For a single taxpayer the same rules are true, except the deduction is phased out for adjusted gross incomes between $25,000 and $35,000.

Do these rules apply if neither spouse is covered by a pension plan?

No. The old rules still apply. A contribution equal to total earned income or $2,000, whichever is lesser, will be allowed for each person, while a married couple with one wage earner can contribute $2,250.

Are there no other tax benefits to IRAs?

The benefits are not entirely gone. Even if you do not qualify for a deduction of the annual contribution, you can still make a non-deductible individual contribution up to the limit.

The earnings of that contribution can then build up tax-free until they are withdrawn. If you withdraw them after retirement, when you are presumably in a lower tax bracket, you have saved some taxes.

What happens if I make non-deductible contributions greater than the allowable amount?

Any contributions exceeding the allowable amount are subject to a 6% penalty.

How do I withdraw from an IRA?

There are essentially three ways to withdraw from an IRA. You may withdraw the money any time before age 59 1/2, and pay a 10% penalty. You may wait until you are age 59 1/2, withdraw the entire amount, and pay taxes on it. Or you may, after age 59 1/2, take distributions in the form of annuity payments based on your actuarial life expectancy.

Are both deductible and non-deductible contributions to an IRA taxed at withdrawal?

No. Non-deductible contributions will not be taxed, nor are they subject to the penalty for early withdrawal. The accumulated earnings of non-deductible contributions will be taxed, however, and are subject to the penalty for early withdrawal.

How does the IRS know which is which at withdrawal?

They assume that each withdrawal consists of both types of contributions, in proportion to the totals in the account.

How do I withdraw from a qualified retirement plan?

You can roll it over into another qualified plan or into an IRA, or you can withdraw it on an averaging basis over a five-year period.

Can I withdraw on a ten-year averaging basis?

Generally, the 1986 tax law has replaced ten-year averaging with five-year averaging. In some instances for some people age 50 or older on January 1, 1986, ten-year averaging still applies.

What are the age limitations on withdrawals from IRAs and self-employed pension plans?

For both types of plans, withdrawals before age 59 1/2 are penalized 10%. IRA withdrawals must begin by April 1 of the calendar year following the year in which you reached age 70 1/2. You must also withdraw a certain amount each year based on actuarial life expectancy, or be penalized. Withdrawal from a self-employed plan must be completed in the calendar year you became age 70 1/2.

Is the 401(k) plan considered a retirement plan?

Yes, it is. Under a 401(k) plan you may contribute up to $7,000 of your salary to the plan and defer income taxes on it. Your employer may make additional contributions on your behalf. The total of the two contributions cannot exceed $30,000 or 25% of your salary.

How are my Social Security benefits determined?

The benefits you will receive from Social Security are related to the amounts you have contributed, but there is not a direct dollar-for-dollar correspondence. The calculations are complex, based on contributions, age at retirement, survivor and dependent provisions, earnings while employed, and cost-of-living increases for people born after 1920.

How are Social Security contributions calculated?

A wage-earner and his employer each contribute 7.15% of up to $43,800 of his yearly wages, beginning in 1987. The ceiling is expected to rise every year. The self-employed must contribute 12.3% of their net income, up to the same ceiling.

Are Social Security benefits taxed?

If you earn more than $25,000 in other income ($32,000 if married and filing jointly), up to one half of your Social Security benefits are taxable.

How can I collect social security benefits?

Social Security provides benefits for retirement, disability, and survivors insurance, but it can be claimed only by notifying your local Social Security Administration office, who will determine if you are eligible.

Will my Social Security benefits pay for a nursing home?

Social Security does not, but Medicaid does offer nursing home coverage.

What nursing home costs will Medicaid pay?

For a qualified person, it will pay in many instances the full cost of nursing home care, including meals and lodging, health care, and other necessities.

How do I qualify for Medicaid?

The granting of Medicaid benefits is based on your financial condition at the time you apply.

Can I put my assets into a trust so that they are not included in my net worth on a Medicaid application?

The use of a "Medicaid trust" was once an accepted way of removing assets from an estate before applying for Medicaid benefits, but that is no longer true. There are still ways to do this, but they involve a complete transfer of property.

Tax-Advantaged
Investments

Introduction

Tax-advantaged investing should be an important part of the high-income individual's investment program. The purpose of such investment is to increase the investor's net worth by reducing his taxes, and yet allow him an actual gain from the investment. These investments are still worthwhile, even thought the 1986 Tax Reform Act reduced the application of their tax benefits.

Aren't tax-advantaged investments a form of tax evasion?

It is simply a way to convert tax dollars into net worth, which is a valid aim. To paraphrase Ben Franklin, activities engaged in by a citizen to prevent the government from confiscating the fruits of his labor are among the noblest endeavors of man.

What kinds of investments make good tax shelters?

The first tax shelter that everybody should have is a retirement plan, be it an IRA plan, a Keogh plan for the self-employed, or a corporate retirement or 401(k) plan. Consider the benefits:

Contributions are deductible, within certain limits. The limits include (among others) level of income from all sources, level of contribution allowed, amount of compensation that can be covered, and the combination of plans (if any) in which you participate.

What your contributions earn for you, whether interest or dividends or capital gains, accumulate tax-free in the plan.

You can invest the money in any number of opportunities and can be as conservative or as aggressive as you want to be with your retirement money.

You can designate a beneficiary for your account should something happen to you prior to your retirement.

When you begin to withdraw from the plan you can spread the payments over your retirement years, thereby reducing your tax liability.

If an investment can reduce my taxes, how can I make money at the same time?

In the broadest sense, a tax shelter is any vehicle that reduces taxes today, but allows dollars to grow. This is true, for example, of an IRA or pension plan. This benefit is called "tax deferral" because an account is earning today, but payment of taxes on those earnings is deferred until later.

Don't other kinds of tax shelters make more money than IRAs in the long run?

We have already discussed the fact that tax-exempt bonds and insurance investment contracts provide shelter for interest or investment earnings. There are tax-shelter investments on which more money may be made if the investor is able and willing to take on additional risk.

Take common stocks. Here the significant tax advantage is that no tax is owed on the appreciation of a security until it is sold. An investor can choose when to incur the tax. Unfortunately, present law taxes 100% of the appreciation.

In order to achieve higher tax-advantaged returns, the high-income investor should investigate limited-partnership offerings.

Under the 1986 tax law, who is a candidate for a limited-partnership investment?

The 1986 tax law established maximum tax brackets of 38.5% in 1987 and 33% thereafter. When state and local income taxes are included, effective tax brackets are even higher. Therefore, limited-partnership investments should be considered by those whose investment income (or some part of it) is taxed at these high rates.

The after-tax returns of those assets can be enhanced significantly by repositioning them into a limited partnership, and using deductions from the partnership to shelter some or all of the earnings of the partnership.

What is the process of tax-shelter investing?

First, sit down with your accountant and project your income for the next several years. Also project the expenses required for your level of consumption. The difference will be the amount you have for taxes, savings and investment.

The next step is to find an advisor who knows about tax-shelter investments and have him develop a portfolio for you. You may find such an advisor through your bank trust department, or by going to a major brokerage house, or to a specialty firm concentrating on tax-shelter investments.

How much of my income should I put into such investments?

The amount you have for investment of any kind is what you have after living expenses. Beyond that, guidelines have been developed that spell out the minimum income and minimum net worth required to allow an investor to participate in a limited-partnership investment.

These minimums vary with the relative risk of the program and the size of the investment required. Their purpose is to exclude investors for whom the risk and illiquidity are not suitable.

A balance among several partnership investments is important, but there is no hard and fast rule that dictates how much is the right amount for all investors and investments.

What are some of the pitfalls of such investments?

First, will it give you the benefits you expect? A new partnership should have an "offering document" that describes the business and the various assumptions that have been relied on to develop the investment. It also describes the accounting techniques used, the sharing arrangement with the partners, and so forth. It usually offers a legal opinion as well.

Your accountant or attorney should review this document so that you can be reasonably sure the partnership will, in fact, get the special treatment the tax laws afford for a tax shelter.

Second, will the venture make money? Tax shelter investments are, by nature, difficult to evaluate. You would want to assess the caliber of the management and look at the track record of the general partner. A good advisor can contribute to this analysis and help minimize the risk.

Finally, will the lack of liquidity from this type of investment have an effect on your future financial needs? Good planning can accommodate this limitation.

What if my advisor is promoting a particular product in which he's got an interest?

It depends on what kind of an interest you mean. You would expect an investment advisor to charge a fee, or a broker to make a commission on sales. But be careful if your advisor is actually connected to the business he's trying to sell you; that is, if he's a general partner, for example. This is a real conflict of interest, and you may not be able to trust his advice. Get a disinterested advisor who has had experience in the field.

Must I plan several years ahead in making such an investment?

Tax-shelter investments tend to have a five- to ten-year life cycle, so you and your financial advisors must develop a financial plan which covers this period.

Here are some examples. In a real-estate venture set up while the building is being constructed, the construction and rental may require a year or two. Then the first set of rent increases phase in over the next two to three years.

At the end of that period, if the property is showing a profit, it is time to sell it so the partners can recoup their investment, plus the increase in net worth of the project.

In oil and gas, exploratory drilling is done the first year to locate a source. In the second year, development drilling is done, that is, drilling a number of wells in the area of the source.

Once the wells are producing, you may be able sell your share of the project at what you hope is a profit, although you might choose to hold onto your interest. Even though it is no longer a tax shelter, you would continue to collect the revenue from sales.

When a limited partnership begins to make money, or is sold at a profit, don't the investors wind up paying taxes anyway?

There are two ways a business can yield profit. One is from revenue or cash flow, such as rental income from real-estate investment or oil sales from an oil-drilling venture. The other kind of profit is appreciation, that is, increases in the value of the business. For example, a building constructed in 1980 for $1 million may be sold in 1990 for $4 million. Of course, these two kinds of profitability are related: if you can earn high rent from a property, you can sell it for a good price.

When a business makes money, the investors do have to pay taxes on their share of the income or of the profit from a sale. But these taxes usually come much later than the investment, and may be paid in cheaper dollars because of inflation. It is also possible that an investor is in a lower tax bracket by then, perhaps after retirement.

There are no such things as good or bad tax shelters, only good or bad investments. Make sure you focus on the investment aspect of any proposal. A tax-shelter investment is part of an overall investment program, not a substitute. Do not limit your investments purely to this category, no matter how attractive they may seem.

Limited Partnerships

How does a limited partnership work?

A partnership requires that there be one or more general partners; there may be one or more limited partners. The general partners promote and manage the business, and are personally liable for all obligations, debts, and cost overruns of the business. The limited partners usually provide the bulk of the capital. Their risk is limited to the funds they have invested.

The profits or revenues of the business are not always shared in the same percentages as the initial investment. For example, take an oil and gas venture where the general partner contributes 10% of the needed capital to start the business. The limited partners contribute the remaining 90%.

But this particular business could be organized so that the general partner receives 25% of the revenues, and the limited partners receive 75%. In this case, you say the general partner has a 15% "carried interest" or "promoted interest," the difference between the percentage he contributes at the outset and the percent of the revenue he receives.

Why would the limited partners agree to those terms?

The general partners bear most of the risk. In most cases, the exposure of the limited partners is restricted to the money they've invested. In addition, the limited partners get the advantage of any tax deductions.

Why invest in limited partnerships?

There are some industries that Congress believes are necessary for the public good, but are not sufficiently attractive investments on their own without help from the government. The primary examples are real estate and oil and gas. Some other less important examples include cattle-raising, equipment-leasing and movie-making.

The government doesn't give these industries direct subsidies; instead, they get special treatment under the tax code. In the early stages they generate "artificial" losses: depreciation in the case of real estate, and intangible drilling costs in the case of oil and gas.

How can depreciation be an artificial loss?

What's artificial is the length of time assigned to depreciation under the tax code. Buildings don't need to be replaced every year. And yet a real-estate limited partnership can claim a portion of the value of the building as a deduction each year, as if the building were losing value at this rate.

At the end of the period artificially assigned as the "useful life" of the asset, an accountant will say the value is zero. But the building is still standing and in good shape and can probably be sold for more than the initial cost.

So the notion that a building actually depreciates in the first years is artificial, since it is likely to appreciate, that is, increase in value during that time period.

What is "intangible" about the costs of oil and gas drilling?

"Intangible" costs are what you pay for without having something permanent to show for it at the end. Examples of intangible drilling costs would include renting a drilling rig or paying for labor. In contrast a "tangible" cost would be, for example, the purchase of durable equipment, such as a pump.

What makes an intangible cost an artificial loss?

In the case of the intangible drilling costs for a successful well, for example, the fact that the business gets to claim the cost of drilling as a tax loss beyond the point where the true cost has been offset by the profits of actually finding oil or gas. In addition, once oil or gas has been struck and the wells are producing, depletion allowances partially shelter the income from taxes.

A good tax shelter is also characterized by deductible expenses, in addition to artificial losses.

How do you measure the rate of return on a limited-partnership investment?

The rate of return can be calculated in a number of ways, using the following variables:
Cash flow paid out from the partnership operation to you.
Sales proceeds distributed to you from eventual disposition of the assets of the partnership.
The time delay between the investment made and payment of the above benefits.
The extent of tax benefits that reduce taxable income from this partnership or other like-kind investments.

The combination of all these variables will produce a measure of the rate of return on the investment and will allow comparison with more traditional investments.

How does a limited partnership differ from other investments?

Limited partnerships have several unique features which can be both good and bad. First, a partnership passes through to all investors their share of any tax benefits that come from owning the underlying asset, be it real estate, natural resources, or equipment. This pass-through may enable an investor to apply the tax deductions against income earned from this investment or other like-kind investments.

Second, the investor's financial liability is limited to the amount of cash actually invested in the program. Other assets cannot be attached if the underlying investment does not work out.

The primary disadvantage is that limited partnerships are highly illiquid; they cannot be sold quickly. Thus, other, more liquid assets must be accumulated before any investment should be made into a limited partnership.

Generally, there are suitability standards that must be met by an investor. These standards relate your net worth and your tax bracket to the risk of the particular underlying investment. Initial investments run in the $3,000 to $5,000 range.

What's the difference between a public registration and a private placement of a limited partnership?

A public registration is offered to a large number of people, and the typical minimum for individual investments is $5,000. A private placement is offered to fewer people but the minimum commitment is larger, perhaps $50,000 to $150,000. However, these larger amounts are usually spread out over a number of years in a staged pay-in.

How can I tell if a particular limited partnership is a good investment?

The most important concern is economic. Will the investment opportunity be able to stand on its own feet without the tax consideration? In other words, is it a good investment? If so, then the tax benefits will make it even better. If not, the tax benefits alone may not justify the investment. Then analyze the partnership aspects by reviewing the offering document in detail.

First, look at the structure. You will be sharing benefits of the investment with the general partner, so study the sharing arrangements to make sure the split is fair.

Second, look at the management. The success of a partnership will depend on the expertise and experience of the general partner.

Third, examine the general partner's prior history. Management may have impressive credentials, but if they have not been able to deliver the benefits expected, what good are their credentials?

What if the business doesn't go as well as expected? Where will the partnership get additional capital? What exposure do I have as an investor?

The worst that can happen to you is that you lose all of your investment, but the business cannot come back to you for more money. If the partnership needs to raise more capital, it looks for more general partners, or it can pledge assets to borrow money from a bank.

Occasionally you will find an assessment feature in the partnership agreement that allows the business to come back to the limited partners for additional contributions, but that's not typical.

Suppose my income goes down and I no longer need the tax shelters I am in. How do I get out?

This is another risk of this kind of investment. Your holdings are less liquid than conventional stocks and bonds. That is, they are harder to sell because there is no "secondary market."

At some point after the major risks are past, some combination of the other partners in the venture would probably buy out your share, since they are already familiar with the project.

If nobody buys out a limited partner who is unable to meet his commitment for future payments, he defaults. For tax purposes, a default is considered a sale at zero. A default may incur significant adverse tax consequences, however.

Do some partnerships guarantee to buy back a limited partner's interest after a certain period of time?

Yes, some do. It's a way of providing liquidity. It is most common in oil and gas. But if a limited partner sells his interest back to the general partners, its value is discounted twice.

The first discount is of future revenues to current value, and the second discount (typically one third or more) is taken for risk, since there is always some risk that the wells will collapse or oil or gas prices will go down. So the buy-out figure will probably be about 40% of future value.

For example: With oil and gas there is typically an initial commitment, say $10,000. Then an additional assessment is often made in the second year. Say that the limited partner is assessed $2,500 in year two. Now he's got $12,500 invested.

If he decides to sell, the general partners would buy him out for $10,000 cash, in exchange for a likely future return of $25,000 over about ten years. So you're usually better off holding on to your share of the business unless you really need the cash.

What happens if I want to give my interest in a partnership to my children? Is that any help to me?

A gift is not going to solve a liquidity problem since you don't get any cash from making a gift. But a gift to your children of your partnership interest can be an excellent way of transferring value and shifting income without incurring the gift taxes you might have to pay on a cash gift. You can see how this works by using the example just described:

The discounted value of $10,000 for $25,000 in future revenues may not be a good price for a buy back, but it establishes a legal value for a gift. The low value will reduce potential gift taxes. If you give your interest to your child, it is treated as a gift of $10,000, but your child can expect $25,000 of future cash flow.

In sum, dad invests $12,500. In year two or three he can give his interest in the partnership to his child, having it treated for tax purposes as a gift of $10,000 but in reality transferring $25,000 of future revenue. If the child is fourteen or older, he or she will be taxed on the income received at a rate that is probably lower than dad's.

However, if the child is thirteen or younger, he or she will pay tax based on dad's rate. As you can see, the age of your child is an important issue if tax reduction is the goal.

Oil and Gas

What's the typical life span of a partnership in oil and gas?

If the venture is successful, cash flow will begin twelve to twenty-four months after the start of the partnership, and will continue for the productive life of the wells. However, the majority of the return will occur in the first seven to ten years.

In addition, some general partners may offer to exchange your interest for cash or for stock in the company. Usually this occurs in or after the third year of operations.

Can companies specialize in just oil or gas or do they always produce both?

Oil and gas usually go together, although some programs have more of one than the other. Since most partnerships provide a mixture of the two, your selection is really only a matter of emphasis.

Isn't oil and gas drilling very risky? What if nothing is found?

The risk of oil and gas drilling is really a mathematical risk, based on probability. You do not invest in only one well. You select a company with thirty or more wells, and a mixture of exploratory and developmental drilling prospects.

With such a balanced program, the usual success ratio is about 50%. By investing modest amounts with several companies, you can spread the risk out over an even larger number of wells.

A second risk involves the prices at which the oil or gas is sold. Since oil and natural gas are commodities, prices vary with supply and demand. Pricing therefore has a significant impact on the economic benefits of the reserves found.

What do you mean by exploratory and developmental drilling?

Exploratory drilling is, by definition, drilling in an area that is more than one mile away from an existing well, even though it may be in an existing field or area of known oil-bearing geology. Developmental drilling, on the other hand, is drilling within one mile of an existing well.

The risks of exploratory drilling are naturally greater. You can expect about a 15 to 20% success rate, compared with the 50 or 60% success rate of developmental drilling. So you need to spread the risk over a larger number of wells.

The advantage of investing in exploratory drilling is that the average cost of acreage is cheap. When you do strike oil or gas, it's very profitable. Developmental drilling entails less risk but yields lower profits.

Real Estate

You have told me almost more than I want to know about oil and gas. What are some of the risks of real-estate investment?

Most of the risks are in the early stages. Time usually bails out good real estate. If it is well conceived and well located, it will usually rent fully and return a good income. But early on you have the primary risks of construction and rental start up.

You can't begin to operate a building before construction has been completed. If construction is delayed, those benefits aren't coming in, and yet the investor has already put in his cash.

The risk of cost overruns is of concern only to the general partner, since the limited partners won't have to put up additional capital.

Next is the risk that the property will not rent as quickly as planned. During the time it is vacant, you lose revenues, and this delays cash distributions.

Are there deductible expenses in a real-estate enterprise that make it a good tax shelter?

Yes. In real estate, the business has interest expenses if it borrows money. It also pays property taxes and, of course, benefits from depreciation. Just as with an individual, these expenses are tax-deductible, but only to the extent that the investor has income from like-kind investments. Otherwise, the losses accumulate and are applied against any future capital gain from sale of the asset, in order to reduce the taxes due upon sale.

Why doesn't this work for stockholders of a corporation?

A tax-shelter investment is in a particular form of business entity, usually a partnership. A corporation in which you own stock keeps its losses and gains to itself. Whether you make money or lose money depends mainly on the market value of the stock at the time you sell. With a partnership, the gains and losses of the business are reported on the income-tax returns of the partners, a process called "pass through."

While there are other forms of direct-participation businesses which allow pass through of tax losses, such as subchapter-S corporations and direct full (100%) ownership, partnerships are the most common form.

What is the typical life-cycle of a real-estate partnership?

An investor commits himself to paying a certain amount each year for a given period.   This is called a "staged" pay-in.   For example, you might commit $10,000 per year for five years, a total of $50,000.

Construction and the initial rental of the space will take place in years one and two.   Then, over the next few years, as the second set of tenants comes in, the rents increase.   By year five, the revenues generated by rents begin to exceed the deductions for depreciation and expenses of the business.

The investment may not really be a tax shelter any more but may have become a profitable business.   At this point, the partnership can simply sell the property.   The partnership is dissolved, the proceeds are distributed, and the partners make a profit treated for tax purposes as a capital gain.

How do real-estate partnerships usually come to an end?

When a property is sold, the mortgage gets paid off first, then the limited partners get their original capital back.   The remaining profits are split between the general and limited partners according to a percentage that reflects the degree of risk taken on by both parties.

In a venture such as new construction, where the general partners take a higher degree of risk, they get a bigger share of the profits when the business is sold.

Is selling the property the only way to cash in?

Another way of getting cash out of a real-estate partnership without dissolving the business is to refinance.   Take out a second mortgage using the property as collateral.   This increases interest payments, creating additional deductible expenses.   Meanwhile, the cash you get from the bank is tax free, since it is neither income nor a capital gain, just a loan.

Insurance

Introduction

According to Will Rogers, being grown up means we can have our own way—at our own expense. Although life insurance can go a long way towards preserving a family's well-being when someone dies, some people are skeptical about buying life insurance—and paying the premiums. Yet surveys show that, on the average and separate from equity in a home, more than 80% of the income-producing assets in the typical estate comes from life-insurance proceeds.

Even when life insurance makes up a smaller proportion of the estate, it is likely to represent a big percentage of the *liquid* assets. Thus, life insurance plays a vital part in the process of planning an estate.

The number of insurance variations and coverages offered today can make the process of selecting the best policy seem very complicated. It need not be.

Why should a person buy life insurance?

Life insurance is simply a way to protect a beneficiary financially when an insured person dies. Typically, a wage-earner buys life insurance to protect his family. This way, he can create an estate that he would not be able to accumulate through savings.

Are there people who really don't need life insurance at all?

Although a younger person without dependents might choose not to buy life insurance, he should bear in mind that his circumstances may change. He will probably get married and have children, and one or both of his parents might become disabled. He will get much better rates if he buys insurance as a younger man, and he is unlikely to have the health problems that could prevent him from obtaining needed insurance later in life.

For an older person with no dependents, life insurance may be unnecessary.

Types of Policies

What are the different types of insurance policies, and what are the advantages of each?

The two basic types of life insurance policies are term or temporary insurance, and permanent insurance. Term insurance lasts for a term of years and then it's over. Only if you die within that term of years is there a payout. The beginning premium cost is very low. The annual premiums for the same policy increase as the insured person gets older.

With permanent insurance, the premium is higher to begin with but does not change, and you can't outlive your coverage.

The choice depends on ability to pay. A young man just starting out with a limited income will probably buy term insurance because the premiums are lower. As his income allows, he switches or converts to permanent insurance later. At the time he switches, he does not have to prove insurability.

If the ability to pay is not a concern and coverage is needed for a long period of time, it's probably wisest for the buyer to start with a permanent policy.

Is "whole life" the same as "permanent" insurance?

"Whole life" is another name for permanent insurance. It is also called "straight life," since the premiums remain constant. "Straight life paid up at age 90," for instance, means the buyer has the right if he wishes to spread out premium payments over the years until he reaches age 90.

What does "retired life reserve" mean?

The employer corporation builds up a side fund which is not taxable to the employee and is deductible to the employer. By the time the employee reaches age 65, the side fund should be sufficiently large to pay the premiums for his group term life insurance until the employee's death.

What do "double indemnity" or "accidental death" mean?

The insurance company pays twice the face amount of the policy if death is due to an accident.

Will a paid-up permanent life policy increase in value?

The cash surrender value of such a policy will increase. Further, if the life-insurance company is a mutual company and dividends are left with the company to purchase additional paid-up insurance, the face value of the policy will increase as well.

Are there policies that automatically keep pace with inflation?

Yes. You can ask for an index protection provision to be added to a policy at a small additional cost. Then, if the cost of living rises, the face value of the policy will also rise.

Do investment or variable life-insurance policies offer inflation protection?

Investment or variable life policies have their death benefits and cash values tied into the investment performance of an underlying portfolio of securities, such as government bonds, corporate bonds or common stocks. This is much like a mutual fund.

Such a policy can provide inflation protection through the long-term growth of the investment account. There is no guarantee that this will be happen, but historically it has.

How should a person decide how much coverage to have?

First, a buyer must determine what the financial needs of his or her family will be if he or she dies. How much income would be needed for the family to live on to maintain a present lifestyle and for how long? Will there be estate taxes due at death? What other final bills must be paid? What should be done about mortgages and children's college education needs?

After determining needs, the next step is to determine what assets are already available in the estate that can be used to provide funds to meet these needs. For example, where does Social Security fit in?

After the analysis comparing available funds against the various needs has been completed, any shortfall can be spotted. Life insurance can then be bought to fill in the gaps.

Finally, the buyer has to assess ability to pay premiums. If cash flow is a concern, the needed insurance may have to be purchased over a period of years.

Premiums

What are the premium costs of different types of life insurance?

The beginning annual premium for a $100,000 term policy is about $145.00 for a male aged 35. The premium will increase over the life of the policy. The annual premium for the same policy as permanent insurance is $1,070.

What do you get for paying the higher premium? First, the payment level is guaranteed, so the difference between the two premiums narrows over the years. Second, equity builds up in a permanent insurance policy. You can borrow against this so-called "cash value," and get it back when you terminate the policy. Also, you can use the dividends on this policy to reduce premium payments further.

What are the various methods of paying premiums?

You can pay annually, monthly, quarterly or semi-annually. If you have a number of policies, you can have your checking account billed monthly for all the policies together. There is a small charge for this, but the extra cost is tax-deductible, and you have the use of your money longer than if you paid all your insurance in one lump sum.

Can an insurance company ever increase premiums?

If the life-insurance company is a mutual company, you receive dividends on the equity you have built up through payments, and these dividends can be used to *reduce* premiums. Don't get rattled by the various terms and payment options. Just remember that with permanent insurance, if you don't change the face amount of the policy or your payment arrangement, the premiums will stay constant.

Does it make any sense to borrow against a life-insurance policy for any reason?

When you borrow money from an insurance company on the cash value of a policy, you use the equity you have built up in the policy to secure the loan. Thus, you don't have to spend earned income and reduce your standard of living for an expense such as educating your children.

Even if you don't have a specific purpose such as education expenses, you can borrow on your life insurance at a low rate. If you invest that money, you can deduct the interest cost of the borrowing, up to the level of investment income from interest or dividends. You offset one against the other. Bear in mind that the borrowing must be repaid, either by you or from the death benefits of the policy.

If I have a paid-up policy and feel fine, shouldn't I just cash in the policy?

Be sure you understand what it means to have a policy "paid up" and what a policy's "cash surrender" value is. These terms apply to permanent insurance only. To have a policy paid up simply means no more premiums are due. If you close out the policy, the cash surrender value is the amount of money the insurance company would pay you.

Whether a person should cash in a policy or not depends on many factors. Is there a continuing need for the protection the policy provides? Are there tax consequences, possible annuity pay outs, and so on? It is advisable to explore all this with a trusted insurance advisor before deciding.

Annuities

What is an annuity?

An annuity is simply an arrangement for a person (called an "annuitant") to pay an amount of money to an insurance company, over a period of years or in a lump sum. In exchange the insurance company promises to pay back later a lump sum with interest, or to make monthly payments for as long as the annuitant lives.

The annuitant pays no tax until payments begin, and then only pays tax on the interest earned, not on the original investment. An annuity may therefore have a higher rate of return than other low-risk investments.

Who should consider buying an annuity?

An older person with money in the bank, concerned about outliving sources of income and who wants to reduce current income taxes. It's a relatively safe investment, you cannot outlive it, and you do not have to manage it.

Since you may be locked into the interest rate at the time you buy the annuity, a period of high interest rates is another reason to buy it. But variable or adjustable-rate annuities allow for changes in interest rates or other earnings in the contract. In so doing, they will change with outside economic conditions and interest rates.

Isn't this the way a lot of pension plans pay retired people?

Yes, it's very similar. The annuity can continue for the life of a spouse as well, passing income to a surviving spouse. But keep in mind that if you are covering your spouse's life as well as your own, the monthly payout is going to be reduced because the same payout is likely to be spread over a longer period of time. This is called a "joint and survivor" life annuity.

Other terms are used to describe annuities. A "non-refund annuity," for example, is a regular monthly income payable for life, but payments cease at death. An installment refund annuity, on the other hand, contains a guarantee to pay back the principal to someone else if death comes before the principal sum is fully paid back.

Insurance and Estate Planning

How important is group life insurance in an estate plan?

The group insurance provided by many companies seems attractive because it is not very expensive. As a matter of fact, most such plans are non-contributory; the company pays the entire premium. But there are limitations.

An employee leaving the job loses group insurance, and at retirement loses all or most of it. If someone has based an entire estate plan on group insurance and suddenly finds himself without it, the plan may be in shreds.

It will be important in the years ahead for employers to consider group life insurance programs that can be extended beyond age 65.

I expect to leave a sizable estate but my holdings are mainly real estate and antiques. How would life insurance help?

Although an estate may be large, it may not be "liquid." The holdings might consist of real estate, stock in a family company, antiques or works of art, or stocks and bonds. To sell an asset like a stock or bond to pay final bills may involve a loss if the market is down, and also loses future growth and income.

A liquid asset can be easily and quickly transferred to cash without suffering a loss in value. Life insurance proceeds fit into this category very well. Typically, a widow or other dependent needs cash when the breadwinner dies, to make up for lost income and to pay estate taxes. Life insurance proceeds can provide the cash, allowing the remainder of the estate to be conserved.

If I leave life insurance proceeds in a trust for my spouse's benefit, is that money available if needed?

A trust can be designed to allow your spouse to have access to the assets. An attorney should be involved in the design of such a trust.

Are life insurance proceeds taxed in my estate when I die?

If you owned the policies, life insurance proceeds are included in your estate for federal tax purposes. To avoid this, someone else should own the policy and pay the premiums; a family member perhaps.

State inheritance or estate taxes vary, so you would have to review the tax laws of your state with your lawyer.

Something else to remember is that a beneficiary does not have to pay income taxes on life insurance proceeds.

Can someone other than the person insured own the policy?

The owner of the policy controls it: he can borrow against it, select and change beneficiaries, cancel or renew. The "insured" (the person whose life is insured) does not have to be the owner. In estates of modest size, it is logical for the insured to be the owner. As the estate gets much larger, however, it might be advisable to have someone other than the insured be the owner. That way, the life insurance proceeds will not be part of the insured's taxable estate, since he did not own the policy.

One way to achieve this separation between insured and owner is for the insured to create a trust, which then owns the policy. The trustees, of course, have control over this policy.

Is there any rule of thumb for deciding the beneficiary of a life-insurance policy?

Usually a person buys a policy and names his or her spouse the first beneficiary. A common problem is that many beneficiaries have difficulty managing the large influx of cash created by life insurance proceeds on the death of the insured.

A better plan for a sizable estate is to arrange that the beneficiary not have primary responsibility for managing the property. Obviously, this would be necessary if the beneficiary is a child. A trust, again, is a very desirable way to get around the money-management problem.

Are there any limits on switching beneficiaries? How do you go about switching?

You can change beneficiaries as often as you want. All you have to do is complete a form provided by the insurance company, and mail that form (with proper signatures) back to the insurance company.

Can a policy have multiple beneficiaries?

You certainly can name multiple beneficiaries. There is nothing complicated about that arrangement. The proceeds are simply divided into the appropriate shares.

Can an insurance company retain proceeds and pay them out over a period of time rather than in one lump sum?

Yes. There are a variety of options available to the beneficiary. The money can be held by the insurance company and interest paid to the beneficiary. Or, the money can be transferred to the beneficiary in equal payments over a period of years, or can be paid during the life of the beneficiary in the form of an annuity.

If the proceeds are not payable under a trust arrangement, the beneficiary can take out a lump sum needed to pay final bills, and leave the remainder at interest until the beneficiary has the time to determine just what his or her income needs actually are. The beneficiary should consult with his or her insurance advisor and other investment advisors on when and how to withdraw insurance funds.

Estate Planning

Introduction

The French novelist Honore de Balzac loved the good things in life, so when an uncle, who was old and stingy, left him a sizable sum, Balzac wrote the good news to friends in these words: "Yesterday, at five in the morning, my uncle and I passed on to a better life." If you have ever benefited from someone passing on "a better life," you do not have to be convinced of the value of estate planning.

What is estate planning?

Estate planning provides for property distribution and the orderly administration of financial and personal affairs after the estate owner dies. It reduces the costs of transferring assets to beneficiaries: probate court costs, for example, and legal fees, gift taxes, and estate taxes. And it reduces income taxes by shifting income and capital appreciation to other family members or beneficiaries.

The hallmarks of a good estate plan are creativity and flexibility. A creative plan takes into account not only legal requirements but also the personalities of the client and client's family. A flexible plan accommodates changing circumstances, since a will or trust may control the disposition of assets thirty or more years after it is written and signed.

The idea of planning for death is very difficult for many people. The process requires dealing with emotional issues that are frequently repressed. When choosing a lawyer to develop your estate plan, you should look for someone who is sympathetic in dealing with these feelings as well as experienced in the legal aspects of estate planning.

How does an estate plan differ from a regular will?

A will is an important element of an estate plan, but not all of it. An estate plan is an overall plan for the transfer of your property and money, both during your life and after your death. The objective is to conserve these assets for your family or other beneficiaries by minimizing the costs of the transfer, while allowing for some flexibility in the use and distribution of these assets.

A will may be all that is required for one person's estate plan. Another person, or the same person at a later date, may need to set up a trust or establish a gift program. In that case, a lawyer would draft documents setting forth the terms of the trust or documenting the gifts.

What are the benefits of estate planning?

A well-conceived estate plan can increase family wealth and put your affairs in proper order. A good estate plan should reflect creativity in addressing your particular and individual needs. It should also be flexible in its design to allow changes in your personal and financial affairs.

The reward you have from having a comprehensive estate plan is the peace of mind that results from knowing that your family and property will be provided for as you desire, rather than left to the decisions of others.

Wills

Why bother with a will?

There are many important reasons for having a will. The most important one is to specify who will get your assets. If you do not have a will, the law in your state will dictate who gets your assets. You may not agree with the particular disposition mandated by that law.

For example, suppose you have a large estate, die without a will, and you are survived by a spouse and two young children. Who inherits your individually owned property?

In some states, approximately one half goes to your spouse, and one half to your children. Then, when your oldest child becomes eighteen, he or she takes one-fourth of your estate, and can use these assets any way he or she wishes. Most eighteen year olds are not qualified to manage a large inheritance.

What are the other important reasons for a will?

One is to tell the probate court who you wish appointed as fiduciaries for your estate. (Technically, you can only nominate fiduciaries in your will; the court has the power to approve and appoint them.)

A **fiduciary** is a person or organization given the duty to care for property for the benefit of another person. For example, **guardians** control and have legal authority over your minor children (who become their **wards**) and their property if you and your spouse both die when your children are young. (Guardianship can apply to any family members not capable of taking care of themselves.) A **conservator** is in charge of a ward's property but not person. **Executors** have legal authority to control your assets while your estate is being administered.

Trustees have legal authority and responsibility for dealing with assets held in a trust before property is turned over to beneficiaries.

Obviously, for these functions you want individuals or organizations in whom you have complete trust and who understand your wishes. A will affords you some control over the selection of fiduciaries.

ESTATE PLANNING

What is a power of attorney?

A power of attorney is granted by one person to another to take certain actions and execute certain documents on the first person's behalf. It can be useful if the person must be out of the country for an extended period, for example. The person granting must be competent to do so.

A "durable" power of attorney remains in force even if the grantor becomes incompetent or unconscious, although it ceases at the grantor's death. Court permission is not necessary in granting power of attorney.

How old must children be not to need a legal guardian?

That depends on the laws of your state. In most states, the age of majority is either 18 or 21. Until a child reaches the age of majority, he or she does not have the legal capacity to deal with estate matters or property.

How should I decide whom to nominate as fiduciaries?

As guardian, you should name someone, probably a relative, who would raise your children according to your standards, and give them the love and attention they need. Guardians receive the money they need from the executors or trustees who are managing the funds of the estate.

Because the executor's function is mostly administrative, a spouse or some family member can be executor alone if capable in business matters. Otherwise, name a professional person or institution to act as co-executor.

In any event, you should select someone who is likely to survive you, someone who is a contemporary or younger. And you should name an alternate in case your first choice is unable to serve. A corporate fiduciary, such as a trust company, is a good choice; they act as executors regularly and are very experienced. Also, the trust company, unlike an individual, has continuity of existence.

Can an executor also be a beneficiary of a will?

Yes. This is often the case when a spouse or other family member is named to be the executor.

Can one person serve as guardian, executor, and trustee?

Yes, certainly. It is wise in such a case, however, to name an alternate to serve in each capacity, in case the first-named person cannot serve or continue to serve.

Can the lawyer who wrote my will also serve as executor?

Yes, and many people make that choice.

Will I save money by making a will?

Saving money by making a will depends on its provisions. Simply having a will does not necessarily save estate taxes. It can save some money because the cost of administering your estate is likely to be less.

When someone dies **intestate** (without a will), the probate court appoints an administrator to control the property. In most states such an administrator must furnish a bond, and the estate pays the bond premiums.

The administrator may need judicial authorization to sell real estate, settle claims, and distribute the estate, all of which will cost the estate additional fees.

Since a will names an executor and generally gives that person broad powers, there is less need for court involvement, with its related fees.

What is the general format of a typical will?

A typical will names fiduciaries, directs the executor to pay last expenses, debts, and taxes, and gives the executor broad power to sell things, borrow money, and generally manage the property.

It then may designate particular bequests to individuals and charities. For example, it might leave real estate to a spouse, certain tangible property to a child, and a cash sum to a hospital or church.

Finally, it directs disposal of the residue, or what is left. This is usually set forth in percentages, since the total value of an estate is not known until the **testator**, the person who made the will, dies. A will may also be used to create a trust.

Are there general guidelines in making a will?

Not really, although most lawyers will probably recommend that the executor be given broad powers within the limits of the law in your state. This will make administration of your estate smoother, but you will want to give careful thought to selecting the right person or institution to designate as executor.

Complications can arise if you decide to leave real estate or a single item of tangible property to several beneficiaries, even though there might be good reasons to do so in a particular case.

Because estate taxes generally are imposed at graduated levels, most estate planners will recommend that a married couple try to equalize their shares of property. This is a hedge on estate taxes; a greater estate tax burden may result if one spouse owned most of the property and happened to die first.

Can I prepare my own will, if it has standard provisions?

It is safer to have an attorney prepare your will. That way, you will be less likely to leave out something important, and you are assured that it is properly signed and thus valid.

How much does it cost to have an attorney prepare a will?

That depends on the kind of will and companion documents you require. Some attorneys charge a flat fee for a simple will. Most charge by the hour for a more complex document. If an attorney quotes an hourly rate, you can then ask for an estimate of the time required.

Don't be shy about raising the issue of cost. You have a right to know what your expenses are likely to be and how they are calculated. You may also wish to compare the charges of several lawyers.

If I decide to write a new will, should I do anything before seeing my lawyer?

You should first prepare an inventory of your property, the assets you own. Divide it into at least three categories: **real estate**, which consists of land and buildings; **tangible property**, which is anything you can touch, such as household furnishings, jewelry, and cars, but not money; and **personal property**, which includes everything else, such as money, stocks, bonds, and insurance.

List all your property in columns by ownership: husband, wife, or jointly owned, and by these general classes: real estate; bank accounts; stocks and bonds; illiquid securities, such as stock in a privately held corporation; life insurance; retirement plans; and tangible personal property.

You should estimate the fair market value of all these assets. You should also list all mortgages, debts, or liabilities of yourself and your spouse.

Why divide an inventory into ownership columns?

Your attorney needs to know who owns what in order to calculate the estate taxes due if either or both of you should die. Then he or she can analyze ways to change ownership in order to minimize estate taxes. Because these taxes are graduated, it is important to balance the respective estates so that both are in the lowest possible bracket.

Sometimes estates are balanced by transferring joint property to one spouse's individual ownership. Another way is to transfer individually owned property to the other spouse, or to make gifts to other family members.

What happens if I move to a state with community property laws?

The laws of these states vary to such an extent that you should consult an attorney in the state to which you move to find out how those laws would affect you. Bear in mind also that once property is classified as community property, it keeps that status even if it is transferred to another state, or if you move to another state.

It is wise to review your estate plan each time you move to a new state to see how your will interacts with the probate and tax laws of that state.

Is there anything else I should do?

You could diagram a family tree showing the names, addresses, ages and relationships of family members. This helps the attorney build flexibility into your estate plan in appropriate ways, and saves time.

It is also a good idea to make copies of certain documents to leave with the attorney, such as deeds to real estate, insurance policies, retirement plans, and existing wills and trusts. These documents are important for reference.

Estate Taxation

Is everything I own subject to estate taxes at my death?

In general, those assets you own or control at the time of your death are subject to federal estate taxes. They include real estate, stocks and bonds, life insurance, and personal property such as household furnishings, cash, and bank accounts.

The fair market value of these assets at the time of your death equals your gross estate, along with one half the value of any property you own jointly with your spouse. Because of the unified credit, however, you may not have to pay taxes.

What is a unified credit?

Tax credits for gifts and for estates, formerly separate, have now been unified into one. A person can use it during life to reduce gift taxes or later to reduce estate taxes. The maximum gift or estate tax forgiven is $192,800.

Another way of stating this is to say that a taxable estate of $600,000 or less has no federal estate tax liability. This amount is called the "exemption equivalent," or "free amount" because it passes free of taxation.

What is the marital deduction?

Property passing to a surviving spouse is exempt from federal tax. To qualify, the property must pass to the spouse, or be held for her or his benefit, and the spouse must have the right to all the income.

How much property qualifies for the marital deduction?

All of it. The internal revenue code allows a 100% marital deduction, no matter how large the estate.

What is a state death tax credit?

A state death tax credit is a credit which is allowed when a federal estate tax return is filed, whether or not an individual's estate is subject to any form of tax at the state level. The credit is based on a mathematical calculation and is not the same as the amount of taxes actually paid.

Will retirement benefits from my company be included in my taxable estate?

Retirement benefits are included as part of a decedent's gross estate, if the company retirement plan provides for survivor's benefits, and if the decedent was entitled to benefits at the time of death.

A participant in a pension plan should also be concerned with the 15% excise tax imposed on "excessive pension accumulations." If the individual dies with such an accumulation, the tax is imposed on the amount considered excessive. Neither the unified credit nor the unlimited marital deduction can be used to offset the tax imposed by this law.

Can property shares be equalized *after* the death of a spouse?

A number of procedures can be adopted to reduce federal estate taxes after death. The principal method is to have a beneficiary of the estate disclaim his or her interest in the estate. For example, suppose a man left his entire estate to his wife. The marital deduction would eliminate any tax liability of his estate.

When his wife dies, her estate would be taxed on the full value of their combined property. To reduce this tax she could, within nine months, disclaim a portion of her interest in her husband's estate. It would then pass on (perhaps to their children) under the other provisions of his will, as if she had predeceased him.

If joint property passes automatically to the survivor, is it taxed?

The good news is that such property is not subject to probate. The bad news is that for federal estate-tax purposes, one half of joint property is usually included in the estate of the deceased owner. State laws vary in their tax treatment of joint property.

Won't my estate save money if I own property jointly?

Normally probate court costs are less for an estate settlement if property is owned jointly. However, joint ownership of property may lead to greater estate tax costs when the surviving joint owner subsequently dies. These additional estate tax costs could be far greater than the savings in probate court costs.

Is there any advantage to owning property individually rather than jointly?

Owning property separately offers the flexibility to control how that property is passed on. A jointly held asset does not pass to a trust, for example, but to the surviving joint owner.

Since jointly held property goes to the survivor, one half may be taxed to the first estate, and all of it remaining in the possession of the survivor is then taxed to the second estate. Thus half is taxed twice.

Separate ownership allows property to be passed to a trust to avoid this double taxation. Whether separate or joint ownership is best depends on individual circumstances, however.

How is the federal estate tax calculated?

First to be determined is the value of the assets that would be included in an estate. Then from those assets are subtracted funeral expenses, any debts and other obligations of the decedent at the time of death, executor's fees, attorney's fees, and probate court costs.

In addition, subtracted from the estate is the amount passing to a spouse (the marital deduction), and any amounts left to charity.

The net amount left is called the taxable estate, and is subject to rates graduated from approximately 37% to 55%, after the unified credit is applied. In 1988, the top rate drops to 50%.

Who actually pays estate taxes, as well as other last expenses, such as medical bills and funeral costs?

These costs, as well as the costs of administering the estate, are normally paid by the executor, from the assets of the estate. A will should specify which portion of the estate is to be used to pay such costs, taxes, and expenses. If this is not clearly set forth, or if there is no will, then the expenses and taxes are paid from various assets according to the laws of the state where the decedent lived at the time of death.

Suppose you willed your daughter a certain sum, but you failed to specify in your will that that sum was not to be reduced by estate expenses or taxes. Depending on the laws of the state with jurisdiction, the bequest to your daughter might be tapped for a share of the expenses and taxes. This is another example of why it should not be left to the state to decide how the assets of an estate are to be distributed.

How are state taxes on an estate computed?

In general, state death taxes are computed at lower rates than are federal estate taxes. Beyond that, the differences among states are extreme.

The term "death taxes" refers to estate taxes and inheritance taxes. The former are taxed to an estate; the latter on bequests to individual beneficiaries.

Some states impose what is known as a sponge tax, which allows the state to collect an amount equal to the federal credit for state death taxes.

Would all of my property be subject to state death taxes?

It is best to review the death tax laws of your state with your attorney. You should also consider the death tax laws of any state in which you own property, which can impose such taxes on that property. For example, if you live in New York and own a summer residence in Massachusetts, the Commonwealth of Massachusetts can tax your estate for the value of the summer home.

If federal estate taxes are much greater than state death taxes, why should I worry about state taxes?

You should be concerned with state death taxes because they can be in fact larger than federal taxes in particular cases. For instance, the unified credit exempts the first $600,000 of an estate; over that amount, the federal tax rate starts at 37%.

A state tax on an estate under, or not significantly over, the $600,000 could be greater than the federal tax. The same could apply to an estate taking maximum advantage of the marital deduction for federal taxes.

If I own real estate in several states, must my will comply with the law of each of those states?

This question brings up two separate issues. First, to be valid, a will must be in accord with the laws of the state where it is signed. But you might reside in a different state when you die. In that case your will, if originally valid, will be valid in your state of residence.

If you own real estate in various states, your will is submitted for probate in each state, and the terms of the will determine who receives the real estate.

What happens if my estate is liable for taxes but it consists mostly of property such as real estate or antiques, with not enough cash to pay the taxes?

Such an estate is called an "illiquid" estate. The executor may sell an asset to raise the cash needed for taxes, or ask the beneficiaries each to pay a share of the tax due in proportion to their bequests. In some cases, life insurance is bought to provide cash for taxes.

A special provision of the tax code provides some relief for estates consisting mainly of closely held businesses, whose stock is not easily cashed in. It allows an executor to spread out the taxes over a long time period, at a low interest rate for part of the deferred tax.

Another special-use valuation provision exists for agricultural real estate, which allows land actually used as a farm to be valued at a lower figure for estate-tax purposes.

Gifts

Besides trusts, are there other ways to reduce estate taxes?

A carefully planned program of gifts can reduce estate taxes. Of course, the financial resources and standard of living of the donor should be closely examined before undertaking a gift program, to ensure that it does not jeopardize the donor's financial security or lifestyle.

The advantages of a gifting program include (1) removing property from your estate to reduce your estate taxes, (2) having the future income from the property pass to the donee, (3) shifting future appreciation of the gifted property to the donee, for the same purpose.

The sooner you give property away, the more value you transfer. Time is a key element.

Are there limitations on the amounts of gifts?

No, except that if you give cash or property worth more than $10,000 to one person in a year, the excess amount is subject to a gift tax, unless you use the unified credit. If you were married and had three children, you could give each child that amount and so could your spouse. You could thus transfer up to $60,000 to your children per year without paying gift taxes.

How much is the gift tax?

The gift tax is graduated at the same rate as the estate tax, approximately 37% to 55%. In 1988, the top rate drops to 50%. But the unified credit can also be used to offset gift taxes, allowing you to pass on up to an additional $600,000 free of tax; thus, in the example above, which involves three children, $660,000 could be transferred. With your spouse's $600,000, the total could be as much as $1.26 million.

How can I ensure that a gift is a gift, for tax purposes?

In general, you must part with control of the property completely. Putting cash into a savings account for your child with your name on it as trustee by which you retain control over it is not a *completed* gift. Likewise, putting property into trust for a child but retaining the right to revoke or amend the trust or withdraw the property from it is also not a completed gift.

If you give someone a tangible asset, such as a piece of furniture or a painting, but it remains with you (say you live in the same household), you might choose to write a memorandum as evidence of the gift, to avoid any confusion about its ownership after your death.

Be aware, though, that the tax authorities may argue that you retained a benefit, and may include the gift in your estate anyway.

I want to give something to my child, who is six. Must I use a trust?

A trust is not your only choice. You can put money into a custodial account under the Uniform Gift to Minors Act. It will be released to your child when he or she reaches the age of legal capacity in your state.

There is a new law that has been enacted in some states known as the Uniform Transfer to Minors Act. That law allows greater flexibility in the kinds of assets which can be transferred to a minor. In addition, the child's access to the property can be restricted until age 21.

There is also a special kind of trust for gifts to young people permitted under the tax code, but the child must be given control at age 21. This is the so-called 2503(c) trust, named after the IRS code section which applies.

If you wish to maintain some control after the child is 21, yet qualify the gift for the $10,000 exclusion, you must include special provisions in the trust document.

Who will be responsible for any income tax assessed on property I give my child?

Your child will be responsible for filing an income-tax return and for payment of income taxes. Moreover, if he or she is below age fourteen and can be claimed as a dependent on your tax return, your child will pay tax at the same rate your income is taxed. This has become known as the "kiddie tax."

It is important to keep in mind that this rule applies to all unearned income, and not just income from property received from a custodial parent.

Does this rule apply to earned income as well?

No. It applies only to unearned income, such as interest, dividends and capital gains. Salaries and income from summer jobs, paper routes, and lawn-mowing is considered earned income, and is taxed at the minor's lower rate.

For individuals with closely held businesses and corporations who wish to spread some income to their minor children, it may be advisable to employ the children and pay them a reasonable salary. Such amounts are taxed at the minor's rates.

Are there any sources of unearned income for which this rule is inapplicable?

Yes. It may be advisable to invest in either tax-exempt municipal bonds or Series EE U.S. Savings Bonds which mature after the child reaches age fourteen. Or consider accumulating the funds in a trust, and distribute the income after the child reaches age fourteen.

You may also wish to consider single-premium life-insurance investment contracts, or growth stocks which do not pay dividends. When making such a decision, you should be aware of your state income-tax provisions and how they apply to these kinds of income.

If I wish to make gifts to my grandchildren, will the same rules apply?

Any unearned income (over the first $1,000) paid to a grandchild below age fourteen will be taxed to the minor at the custodial parent's rate, regardless of the source.

In the case of gifts to grandchildren, there is a generation-skipping transfer tax to take into account. This tax generally applies to certain transfers to a person who is two or more generations removed, such as a grandchild or great-grandchild. The tax is imposed at a 55% rate for 1987 and a 50% rate for 1988 and beyond.

Should I rewrite my will because of this tax?

You should at least review your current will with these and other provisions of the law in mind. But there are certain exceptions to the generation-skipping transfer tax of which you should be aware.

First, any transfer which falls within the $10,000 gift exclusion or is a transfer for education or health-care purposes is not subject to the new tax.

Also, a person with an estate of $1 million or less does not have to be concerned with this tax, because anyone may make cumulative $1 million lifetime and testamentary transfers and not be subject to the tax.

In addition, a person may also transfer up to $2 million to each grandchild prior to January 1, 1990, without imposition of the tax.

Hasn't this tax been around a while?

The current tax dates from 1986. An earlier generation-skipping tax was enacted in 1976, but it was repealed retroactively to that date, and any tax paid under the old law will be refunded to the executor of an estate upon application to the IRS.

Trusts

What is a trust, and why is it useful?

A trust is a written document in which a person transfers legal title to property to a person or institution and instructs that person or institution to use the property for the benefit of a third person.

The person who establishes the trust is the **grantor**, also called a "donor" or "settlor." The one who invests the property and carries out the grantor's instructions is the **trustee**. The **beneficiary** is the person who benefits from the property. These are the basic elements of a trust, although there are many others.

A trust created under the terms of a will is called a **testamentary** trust. A trust created by a person during lifetime is called a **living** trust or **inter vivos** trust. A living trust, in coordination with a will, can do all that a testamentary trust could do.

Two major reasons to use a trust are to provide control over property and to shelter property from estate taxes.

Why would a trust grantor want to prevent a beneficiary from having control over property?

Generally because the beneficiary is judged not to be capable of managing the property. For instance, minor children orphaned by the death of both parents could benefit from the help of a trustee to manage their estate until they reached an age, specified by the grantor, deemed sufficiently mature to manage it themselves.

Or suppose the beneficiaries are elderly parents who have been supported by a child who died before them. A transfer into a trust created by the child rather than outright inheritance might be in their best interests.

What are the relative merits of setting up a trust while I am alive compared to creating one in my will?

A testamentary trust (one created by a will) is subject to the scrutiny and approval of a probate court. Because of this, the identity of the beneficiaries and the nature and value of the assets are a part of the public record.

Also, the court has the power to review and approve the accounts that the trustee of a testamentary trust must file. The preparation and approval of these accounts can create additional expenses for the trust.

By contrast, a living trust is free from regulation by a probate court and is not a matter of public record. For these reasons, most people prefer to create living trusts.

What are the tax effects of putting property into a trust?

A trust can shelter property from estate taxes, but not from income taxes. Usually, for property in a trust to be excluded from federal estate taxes, the trust must be irrevocable (one you cannot revoke or change), and you must have no control over the assets.

Just putting a bank account in your name as trustee for your child, for example, will not exclude that asset from your taxable estate.

The terms of the trust document for any property you already have in a trust should be reviewed to determine if the property will be included or excluded from your taxable estate.

Why not put all of the property in a trust?

The ideal estate plan takes advantage of both the unlimited marital deduction and the unified credit equivalent amount of $600,000.

If all the property were left to a trust so as to qualify for the maximum unified credit, but has no provision to take advantage of the marital deduction, the estate does not get the optimum tax benefits.

By contrast, suppose you leave all your property outright to your spouse. If your spouse dies soon after you do, the same property will be included in her or his estate for tax purposes.

Using the marital deduction may have kept the property from being taxed in your estate. However, your estate might not have used the unified credit available. Therefore, the second estate may pay more tax than would otherwise be required.

How could I avoid paying more tax than necessary?

Instead of leaving all of your property outright to your spouse, suppose you left some of it in a trust that you created for your spouse's benefit.

The executor of your estate could fund that trust in an amount equal to the credit equivalent, or $600,000. Your spouse might receive income and principal from the trust during her or his lifetime, but would not have complete control over the property.

What is the result?

Because your spouse does not have control, the property is not included in her or his estate at death, and because the trust amount does not exceed $600,000, no tax is paid on this property by the estate of the first to die. In this way, the trust shelters a part of your estate from taxation in your spouse's estate.

If I set up a trust for the benefit of my child, who is under age fourteen, does the income get taxed to my child at my rate?

Yes, it does in some instances, but this depends upon the type of trust you use. If the trust provides that all income will be distributed to your child, then the amount will be considered unearned income to your child and will be taxed at your rate.

However, if your child does not need the current income, it would be advisable to accumulate the income in the trust and distribute it to your child at age fourteen, or later. Under this arrangement, up to $5,000 of income would be taxed in the trust at the lower 15% bracket rather than at the higher 28% bracket.

May I or my wife serve as trustee of a trust for my children, or must I use a bank or an outside person?

In many instances, if you or your wife serve as a trustee, you retain control over the trust, so the income will be taxed to you. Furthermore, if you establish a trust which contains reversionary provisions, such as a Clifford or Spousal Remainder Trust, the income from these trusts will also be taxed to you.

Under a carefully drafted trust document employing a bank or an independent person as a fiduciary, income will not be taxed to you, but you will not retain the same control over the trust you or your wife would have if you or she served as trustee.

How do trusts pay taxes?

To the IRS, a trust (other than a revocable grantor trust) is another taxpayer, just as is a partnership, a corporation, or an individual. It must file its own tax return, and make quarterly estimated tax payments.

Additionally, in accord with the 1986 tax law, most trusts are required to report to the IRS on a calendar-year basis, and the income-tax rates for trusts are nearly identical to those which apply to individual taxpayers.

Estate and Trust
Administration

Introduction

Woody Allen once said that he wasn't afraid of dying, he just didn't want to be there when it happened. That says in a nutshell what everybody thinks about estates and trusts. The subject is closely connected with death, and even though we will each have an estate and perhaps a trust to be administered, we will never be directly involved.

In spite of the emotional negatives, estate and trust administration is a subject which stimulates lively discussion, probably because everyone knows someone who got involved in an estate or a trust, and became confused because he was unprepared for what he found.

What are the immediate, practical tasks to be done if there's a death in the family?

Notify family and friends first. It is wise to accept offers of help with children or household chores. In most states, the next of kin can authorize an autopsy if one is requested, and make funeral arrangements.

Early on, locate the will and other important papers such as life-insurance policies. Most wills do not specify funeral arrangements, but be sure to check. As soon as practical, make an appointment with the bank or law office that will administer the estate.

How would I go about locating the will?

Most law firms that draft wills also offer to store the original. Usually a copy is given to the client for his own files or safe-deposit box, along with a cover letter saying where the original is. So begin with the person's files. If you need access to a safe-deposit box, you can get court permission to do so.

If a bank is named as an executor, the bank will probably have either the original or a copy.

Families should make a practice of keeping wills, insurance policies and other important documents together in a safe place so that they are easy to find.

84

Who decides which lawyer is going to do the legal work involved with the estate?

The executor, or executrix (feminine form of executor), has the right to select and hire a lawyer, as well as other professionals such as investment advisors or accountants, to manage the estate. The person nominated in the will as executor must be appointed by a court, but as a practical matter that person will have to select a lawyer or a bank officer to begin the process.

The executor is a fiduciary appointed by a court, and a fiduciary is someone who executes certain responsibilities for another's benefit. These duties involve the highest degree of trust, confidence and confidentiality.

Basically, the executor stands in place of the decedent. His responsibility is to preserve the estate so that creditors can be paid. Then, after debts and taxes are paid, he distributes the estate's assets according to the terms of the will.

Assuming I am an executor, how do I go about selecting a law firm?

You should look for an office that does estate administration on a regular basis, and which is located in the same state as the majority of the estate assets. Often this will be the same law firm that drafted the will. But you are free to retain someone else if you believe another office will give you better service.

If a bank or other institution is named as executor, the individuals connected with that institution will select a lawyer when legal services are required. Quite often the institution will select the law firm that drafted the will.

After I find the will and contact a lawyer, what will I have to do to manage the decedent's affairs?

You will have the responsibility of conserving and investing the assets in the estate. You must take whatever action is necessary to preserve the value of the property.

At the outset, make sure that property such as real estate has adequate insurance. Locate insurance policies and call the insurance agent to increase the amount of the policy if you need to.

Other assets, such as a business, may also lose value unless you take additional action to provide proper management. In some estates there may be perishable assets, such as farm crops, which will need to be sold quickly or lose all value.

What if the decedent's family needs cash for day-to-day living expenses?

If there was a joint bank account, the survivor may use the funds in the account as his or her own. Family members should apply for the proceeds of a life-insurance policy on which they are named as beneficiaries. If they wish, they may ask the lawyer for the estate to process the applications.

It may take 30 days before those funds are received. If the family needs additional funds, they must get the executor's approval.

You should also be aware that creditors are accustomed to waiting longer than usual for bills to be paid if there's been a death in the family.

Sometimes people ask about using the decedent's car. Immediate family, or others with the executor's permission, may use the car. But the insurance company covering the car should be notified.

Generally, executors do all they can to permit the lives of beneficiaries to continue as is, so long as performance of the executor's fiduciary duties aren't jeopardized.

What about other expenses, such as for insurance or managing a business?

The executor may use his discretion in deciding what expenses to incur in order to best preserve the value of the estate's assets. This would include such expenses as property and casualty insurance, attorney's fees, broker's fees, and business management fees.

Wills and Probate

What does it mean to "probate" an estate?

In essence, "probate" refers to the legal process by which a decedent's will is proven to a court to be his last will and testament. Each state has its own laws governing what happens to a person's property when he or she dies. Usually a special branch of the state court system called the "probate court," and in some states the "surrogate court," is designated to enforce those laws.

The law generally provides that some person, or some organization such as a bank trust company, must petition the court to accept the will as valid and authentic and to appoint the petitioner as executor. The process of gathering and making an inventory of the assets, paying taxes and debts, overseeing distribution and obtaining the court's approval of these actions is what is known as probating the estate.

Does probating a will mean that everything becomes a matter of public record?

After a person's death, his or her will becomes a public document and goes on record at the probate court of the county of the decedent's residence. "Probate assets," those which pass to beneficiaries according to the terms of the will, are also a matter of public record. The executor's accountings are also public record, so anyone can find out the fees he charged.

Assets which do not pass according to the will, such as joint property, contractual benefits like life-insurance proceeds, and property held in trust for the decedent's benefit at the time of his death, will pass outside of the will. Because they are not "probate assets," they are not a matter of public record.

Suppose a person dies without a will? What is the probate process like in that case?

If the deceased dies without a will, the court would appoint someone to carry out the property management and distribution function of the executor. That person is called the administrator, or administratix, if a woman.

What would happen to my assets if I died without a will?

A person who dies without a will is said to die "intestate." The property will be inherited by your family and relatives according to their degree of relationship to you and in the proportions provided by the law of the state of your domicile. This is all spelled out in the statutes of each state. If you have no relatives, all your property is taken by the state.

I am told that two years or more is not an unusually long time for an estate to be probated. If that's true, why does it take so long?

Assets may be difficult to collect quickly. The deceased may have been receiving installment payments for property being sold, for example.

Assets may be difficult to appraise: the value of illiquid items such as stock in a closely held corporation may be the subject of dispute between the IRS and the executor. Assets such as real estate or antiques may have to be sold in order to divide the estate among heirs, and this can take time.

Claims against the estate may require action by a court. Executors once had a reputation for liquidating assets like houses, cars, and collections at fire-sale prices just to be rid of the aggravation. Now they're more likely to try to get a better deal for the estate, and that can take time.

Finally, tax returns must be prepared, filed and accepted by the state and the Internal Revenue Service. A tax audit can add to the time that it takes to close an estate.

What are the costs associated with the probate process? In particular, how much will an executor or administrator be paid?

Probate costs include insurance premiums, commissions on the sale of stock or real estate, property taxes, and so on. Obviously these costs vary, depending on the nature of the assets.

Those people who help administer the estate, such as the executors, administrators and attorneys, are paid for their services at hourly rates, or as a percentage of the value of the assets in the estate. Generally, court costs and executor's fees and attorney's fees run between one and five percent of the value of the assets in an estate. (Sometimes an executor who is also a friend or relative, and perhaps a beneficiary of the estate as well, will refuse a fee.)

Is property taxed differently if it passes "outside" a will?

Definitely not. Property passing under the will is simply property whose disposition is governed by the terms of the will. Some examples of property which pass "outside the will," yet may well be taxed in the estate, are life-insurance proceeds, retirement-plan assets, assets of a trust (depending on the type of trust), and jointly held property. Property that passes under the will and property subject to taxation are unrelated categories.

What's the difference between an heir and a beneficiary?

A legal heir is a person who would receive property from an estate by law if there were no will; basically, he's a relative of the deceased. A beneficiary is a person who receives property from an estate.

A legatee is a person who receives personal property under a will, for example, furniture, clothing, or jewelry. A devisee is a person who receives real estate under a will.

These terms are often used interchangeably, although in a strict legal sense they are different.

Trusts

What is a trust?

A trust is a relationship in which one person, called the "grantor," or "donor" or "settlor," transfers legal title from himself to another person, called a "trustee," and directs the trustee to use the transferred property for the benefit of yet a third person, who is called the "beneficiary."

Trusts are an old method of holding property, and the concept of trusts has existed for centuries. They started before many people could read or write. So the name "trust" really meant just that. A grantor really had to trust his trustee.

Now, most trusts are supported by a written document which sets out the trustee's duties and powers. The grantor must sign the document, and the trustee must accept his appointment as the trustee.

A grantor still must have a lot of faith in the person or organization he selects to be his trustee, although the grantor can retain the right to revoke or amend the trust document.

Do I have to have a lot of money before I should consider setting up a trust? What are some of the reasons people put money into a trust?

The need for a trust does not always relate to the amount of money or other property to be placed in the trust. Trusts are used for property management or tax saving or for both reasons.

In general, the trust mechanism allows property to be managed for someone's benefit by an objective manager. It is useful in situations where the beneficiaries are uninterested in managing the money for themselves, or are unable to do so because they lack experience or legal capacity, as in the case of minors.

You should compare the benefits of a trust with the costs of creating and administering it. Many of the financial benefits associated with large trusts are in the form of tax savings.

What is a grantor trust?

Generally, a grantor trust is a trust created by a person during his lifetime. The grantor is also a beneficiary of the trust and he has the right to revoke the trust or amend its terms. This form of trust is sometimes also called a revocable living trust.

There is no income-tax or estate-tax advantage to this kind of a trust. The income is taxed as if the grantor held the property outright. For estate-tax purposes generally, property held in a grantor trust is included in the decedent's gross estate as though the decedent held the property in his own name.

As long as the grantor has legal capacity to deal with his property, a grantor trust gives him the same degree of control and flexibility as if there were no trust at all. If the grantor becomes incapacitated, however, and can't manage his own affairs, the trust provides on-going management for the trust assets for either a long or short period of time.

The use of a grantor-type trust also avoids the probate court procedures for appointing a guardian or a conservator. This avoids a lot of red tape and legal expense.

A grantor trust can continue to exist for the benefit of others after the grantor's death. For that reason, a grantor trust, or revocable living trust, is the foundation of many estate plans. It offers maximum flexibility and protection without requiring that the grantor give up control over his property during his lifetime, and provides for an orderly disposition of his property at death without the costs and burdens associated with probate.

Are there trusts which cannot be changed?

An irrevocable trust is one which no one has the power to revoke. The only way the trust will cease to exist is by the terms of the trust document itself. (A revocable trust is one that can be revoked by someone, ordinarily the grantor. Of course, revocable trusts become irrevocable after the person who had the power to revoke dies.) Once irrevocable trusts exist, they cannot be revoked, but they can be terminated by the trustees paying or distributing all the property in the trust to the beneficiaries.

People placing money in an irrevocable trust must be very sure of what they're doing, because they cannot change their minds afterwards. There are tax advantages, however. Irrevocable trusts are taxpaying entities separate from their grantors. Also, the assets in an irrevocable trust will probably not be subject to estate tax when the grantor dies.

How is an irrevocable trust administered while its grantor is still alive?

It's administered according to its provisions, just as if the grantor were deceased. The trustee simply manages the assets and keeps records, and pays out trust income or principal according to the grantor's directions in the trust document.

I've heard people talk about a Clifford trust. What is it designed to accomplish?

A Clifford trust is irrevocable, and must last for more than ten years from the date of its creation or until the beneficiary dies. The income is paid to someone other than the grantor, and the principal reverts to the grantor or his estate after the termination of the trust.

Clifford trusts were often used to spread taxable income among family members in order to lower the overall tax rate. The sad news is that the 1986 tax law stopped the tax-shifting usefulness of Clifford trusts and such related devices as spousal remainder trusts through two major changes.

The first is the so-called "kiddie tax," by which all unearned income in excess of $1,000 of a minor below age fourteen is taxed to the child, but at the custodial parent's marginal tax rate, if it is higher. Before this change, income could be shifted to a child who would pay tax on it in a lower bracket than the parent, thus realizing a tax saving for the family.

The second change concerns reversionary clauses in a trust. Formerly, if a trust lasted for ten years before reverting to the grantor, or reverted to the grantor's spouse at any time, the income during the period of the trust was still taxed at the rate for the beneficiary. Now, in general, if a trust has such reversionary clauses, the trust income will be taxed to the grantor.

Don't some trusts have provisions to limit the discretion of a beneficiary?

Yes. They are called "spendthrift" provisions, designed to prevent a trust beneficiary from assigning his or her interest in a trust as collateral for a loan or selling it for cash. The provision is placed in the trust document by the grantor.

Here's how a problem could develop without such a provision. A beneficiary who is to receive income from a trust during his lifetime, but no principal, might borrow cash using his trust interest as collateral. Then the beneficiary would spend the proceeds of the loan and have no money to repay the loan other than the future income from his trust interest. Worse yet, a beneficiary might actually sell his future income.

Grantors often create trusts for family members specifically aimed at preventing them from exhausting their inheritances and leaving themselves destitute. A spendthrift provision in a trust document is intended to keep a beneficiary from defeating the grantor's purpose in creating the trust.

Can a person put his house in a trust?

Yes. It's fairly common for a husband and wife who are in their second marriages. One may own the residence in separate name and not want to put the house in joint name. (The owner may have children to whom he or she wants to leave the house.) But the owner, say the husband, wants his wife to live in the residence as long as she wishes, if she survives him. So he places the residence in a trust, giving his wife the right to live there for the rest of her life. At her death, the house passes free and clear of trust to the beneficiaries.

The trust should have a clause authorizing the trustee to hold and own real estate, and the trustee should also have cash available to him to maintain the residence, pay real-estate taxes, make repairs, and so on, unless the surviving spouse expects to pay those expenses.

Generally, real estate is put into a so-called nominee trust, which is created to hold real estate for the benefit of a grantor's trust. The advantage is that only the nominee trust need be recorded publicly, not the entire trust document, thus affording privacy to the grantor and beneficiaries.

Can a business be put into a trust?

Yes, especially if the owner(s) want to preserve the business for a family member until he is seasoned enough to take it over.

When a person places a business in a trust, he must be very careful about selecting a trustee. The trustee holds legal title to all the trust's assets, including shares of stock in the business, and has the right to vote those shares or sell them.

Anyone considering placing a business interest in trust should also give clear directions in the trust document about who is to manage the business, who's to be on the board of directors, and who has primary responsibility for policy decisions.

Also, the trust should have enough liquid assets so the trustee won't be under pressure to declare a dividend from the business if the beneficiaries need income.

These and other potential problems should be thought through well in advance of the time that the trustee would have to serve.

Can a trust be used to benefit a charity and also get income-tax deductions?

All trusts have two "interests." There is the present beneficial interest enjoyed by whoever receives income or principal from the trust currently, and the "remainder" interest, which is held by whoever will receive the trust's accumulated income and principal when the trust terminates.

It is as if one person could withdraw the interest on a savings account (that would be the present-income interest) and a different person could close the account at some specific time in the future (that would be the remainder interest).

Sometimes a person will put property in trust and receive income from the trust as long as he lives, with the remainder, all that's left in the trust when he dies, to go to a charity. This is called a "charitable remainder trust." The person who creates such a trust gets a charitable deduction for income tax purposes equal to the present value of the remainder interest the charity will get in the future.

Or he could set up a trust whose income would go to charity for a period of years, after which the principal would go to a family member. This is called a "charitable lead trust," and the present value of the income interest is deductible for income tax purposes.

Charitable remainder trusts and charitable lead trusts must be very carefully drafted in order to comply with guidelines set out in the Internal Revenue Code. If you are interested in such trusts, consult an attorney to see to it that they're prepared properly.

What are "spray" powers in a trust?

If a trustee has the power, or is permitted, to distribute trust income or principal among several beneficiaries in unequal amounts, based on his evaluation of their need, the trust is said to have a "spray" provision. The trustee can pay all the income or principal to one of several beneficiaries, or pay it equally to each beneficiary, or pay unequal amounts to each beneficiary. It's up to the trustee.

In deciding what to pay, the trustee considers the competing needs of all beneficiaries and their relative income-tax brackets. Obviously, spray provisions allow a great deal of flexibility in the distribution of property held in trust.

Trustees

How is a trustee appointed?

When a person creates a trust, he names the trustee in a written trust document which he signs. He may also appoint successor trustees, particularly if the initial appointees are individuals who themselves may die or become disabled before the trust terminates. That wouldn't be necessary with a bank trustee, of course. A trust may have as many co-trustees as the grantor wants. Usually, there aren't more than two or three trustees serving at any one time.

How does a bank function as a trustee?

There is an administrative function and an investment function to be performed by a trustee, so banks usually assign both an administrative officer and an investment officer to each account. Each officer is supported by a staff of specialists.

The administrative officer deals with disbursements and discretionary payments from the trust, and is responsible for keeping the records and paying taxes. The administrative officer is also the main contact with both the grantor (if he's still alive) and the beneficiary. He keeps track of changes in the beneficiary's needs and objectives, and he communicates these needs regularly to the investment officer.

It's the job of the investment officer to invest trust assets according to the powers granted by the trust document and to satisfy the beneficiary's requirements.

How does the investment officer at a bank decide what to invest in?

All banks have an orderly process for making investment decisions. Several committees specialize in economic analysis and selecting investments. With their input, the individual investment officer decides what assets to buy, sell or hold in a particular account.

Trust investment officers are usually more interested in protecting against loss or achieving gains in line with inflation than they are in risking great loss in the hope of great gain. Their general guidelines are diversification, safety and liquidity.

Does a bank trust company manage the money or stocks in a trust separately or in a common fund?

Most large bank trust departments have created funds which commingle the assets of several small trusts. "Common trust funds," as the commingled assets are called, are like mutual funds. Common trust funds may be comprised of all common stocks, all bonds (either taxable or tax-exempt), or a mix. The investment performance of common trust funds is available to the public as a matter of law.

Common trust funds are typically used for trusts which have asset values of less than $200,000, because the trustee could not otherwise achieve prudent investment diversification. Common trust funds, like mutual funds, are managed to meet the published objectives of the fund itself, rather than the objectives of the individual shareholders. A small trust may hold a share of several common trust funds, rather than just one.

What kind of limits are there on a trustee's investment decisions?

The limits are set by provisions in the trust instrument and by the "prudent man" rule. That rule says a trustee's investments should be those that a prudent man would have made under the same circumstances.

As a practical matter, trustees prefer to keep the majority of trust assets in what we call "liquid" assets, stocks, bonds and cash, rather than in investments such as real estate and shares of closely held businesses. Most trustees, particularly institutional trustees, have relatively little experience in those latter types of investments.

Also, stocks, bonds and cash investments permit the trustee to sell investments that don't go well, and to alter investment strategy if circumstances change. Less liquid investments do not usually have that kind of flexibility.

What powers should I give my trustee?

A trust document tells the trustee how he is to pay out trust income and distribute principal. It also tells him what investments he's empowered to make. Generally, a trustee should be given broad powers.

For example, a trustee may be permitted to pay trust income or principal among one or several beneficiaries, based entirely on his assessment of their needs. Or he may be given the power to retain income for future payment.

A trustee might be limited to certain types of investments. But because trusts and trustees must deal with future events, it's usually better to give them broad investment powers so they can deal flexibly with whatever confronts them.

What are the advantages and disadvantages of choosing a nonprofessional, such as a friend, to serve as a trustee?

Some people feel more secure knowing that their financial matters are being handled by someone who is a close family friend or relative. But the most important qualities a trustees should have are experience and sound judgment. They should also have access to solid investment research, knowledge of legal requirements, and the ability to make necessary and difficult decisions.

What if I appoint a friend or relative I trust, but who does not know all the ins and outs of being a trustee?

If you choose an individual inexperienced in these matters as a trustee, you should also nominate someone experienced in them as a co-trustee. Another reason is that two heads are better than one, and several specialists can do a better job than one generalist.

Unless the trust document states otherwise, co-trustees have equal responsibility for all decisions and must make those decisions unanimously.

A person may believe that although a large institution has experience and is efficient, it lacks personal warmth. In such cases, he may name a close personal friend, a trusted attorney, or a particularly objective family member to serve as individual trustee with a bank co-trustee.

The individual acts as the major contact with beneficiaries. The presence of an individual trustee, particularly just after the grantor's death, often supplies a measure of comfort to beneficiaries, who might be anxious about dealing with a bank acting as trustee.

How much do trustees charge?

Fees are generally computed as a percentage of both the value of the property held in trust and the income it produces each year. If the value of the trust's assets and income go up (or down) then trustee fees will also go up (or down).

As a rule of thumb, fees charged by bank trustees are presently about one percent of the market value of the trust's assets. For example, a bank trustee of a trust with a market value of $300,000 would receive annual fees of $3,000. For larger trusts, most banks reduce the percentage.

Also, there may be a termination fee charged by the trustee; such fees may be computed at the rate of 1% to 2% of the principal value of the trust.

Trustee fees compensate them for spending time investing and supervising assets, for keeping accurate records, for making necessary tax filings, and for assuming the financial liability that goes with being a fiduciary.

Bank trustee fee rates are public information. Individual trustees, such as lawyers, do not publish their rates, but it would be reasonable to assume that they are about the same as bank fees.

Could I be my own trustee for a trust that I set up?

Yes. One of the reasons you might want to be your own trustee is that it would be a good way for you to mange your own affairs, and at the same time, have your property already in trust. If you were to die, the assets of the trust would avoid probate.

This is a useful way to set up estate plans for elderly people, for example, who do not want to pay trustee fees. If you do decide to be your own trustee, make certain that you're working with an experienced professional advisor.

I agree with Woody Allen. I don't want to be there when it happens. How can I know that my trust is in good hands?

If you want theological or philosophical reassurance, you won't find it here. But bank trust departments all publish educational literature, and all employ people skilled in explaining the services they offer. They do this at no charge. Take advantage of it.

Second, don't let your lack of familiarity with the jargon of trust and estate administration prevent you from developing a good estate plan. You may not benefit yourself, but a properly planned and administered estate or trust will ease the minds of those you love at a time when they are likely to need it most.

Case Study:
Moderate-Income
Family

Introduction

In the words of the Roman historian Livy, "Seldom are men blessed with good fortune and good sense at the same time." The case studies that follow are demonstrations of our effort to take Livy's advice, by convening roundtable discussions of typical planning teams to apply the con-cepts presented in this book to appropriate family situations.

We recommend such a roundtable forum for your planning, because it offers you the chance to interact with your team of advisors in the process of developing your financial and estate plan. Our case study method is a hands-on approach which combines the various areas of financial planning into one comprehensive set of goals and objectives. The advice which is contained within each case study provides a broad range of answers to some of the more commonly asked questions in the financial planning area.

The first case study concerns a hypothetical family of moderate means. The Millers are at a significant turning point in their lives. In the next few years, they will make many important financial decisions regarding investments, education of their children, and their own retirement.

The purpose of discussing their financial and personal situation is to illustrate how a team of professional advisors would develop a financial plan, prepare you to ask the right questions during your meetings with your advisors, and offer you enough background to evaluate the answers you receive.

What income and expenses do the Millers' have?

Alan and Nancy Miller are both in their early forties. Alan is an assistant manager of a large division of a national company. Last year he earned $45,000, but he says that his income can vary by about $5,000 either way, depending on his bonus.

His job prospects are bright and he expects to advance in the company and receive increases in salary.

Nancy works part time in the sales department of a small retail store and expects to earn around $15,000 this year. It is unlikely that her income will increase substantially in the next few years.

The Miller's major family expenses include monthly mortgage payments, real-estate taxes, food, clothing, heating costs, and expenses related to their cars. Living expenses consume all but about $5,000 of their yearly after-tax income.

How much property do the Millers have?

The Miller home is presently worth about $150,000 but has a mortgage of $70,000 outstanding. The equity is, therefore, about $80,000. They recently bought a summer cottage, and have about $15,000 equity in that property. They own both houses jointly.

They have stocks worth approximately $10,000, and about $10,000 in a money market fund, all held jointly. Alan also has company stock options, currently worth about $75,000. Since the stock would cost Alan $25,000 to buy, the net value of the options is $50,000.

Alan's tangible personal property (automobiles, furniture, a stamp collection, and some other things) is worth about $15,000. Nancy owns some antiques, silver and jewelry that she estimates as worth about $10,000.

Summary of Assets Of Alan and Nancy Miller

	Alan's Property	Nancy's Property	Joint Property
Home (net of mortgage)			$ 80,000
Summer Home (net of mortgage)			$ 15,000
Money Market Fund			$ 10,000
Marketable Securities			$ 10,000
Tangible Personal Property	$ 15,000	$ 10,000	
Stock Options (net benefit value if exercised)	$ 50,000		
Group Life Insurance	$100,000		
Whole Life Policy	$ 50,000		
Retirement plan	$ 60,000		
Totals	$275,000	$ 10,000	$115,000
Combined total:			$400,000
Potential inheritance:	$150,000	$150,000	

Who else is in the family?

Alan is an only child. His father is deceased. His mother has about $150,000 worth of assets. Alan and Nancy have two children. Their son, Frank, is sixteen and their daughter, Martha, is fourteen. Nancy's father is living, and can support himself without financial help.

Nancy's mother passed away recently, and her will is now being probated. The size of Nancy's mother's estate is about $500,000. Nancy has a brother and sister, so the $500,000 from her mother divided by three might make a $150,000 inheritance for her.

Tax Planning

How can the Millers minimize their current income taxes and increase their cash flow?

The 1986 tax law is intended to promote the efficiency of the economy by causing individuals to make investment decisions more on the basis of economic merit than on the basis of the tax benefits.

In keeping with this new philosophy, there are several tacks which the Millers may take, including rental of the summer cottage. The IRS imposes some limits regarding the number of days the Millers will be able to use the cottage themselves and still create a tax loss from certain expenses such as depreciation, maintenance and utilities.

The tax law will not treat as personal use the days where the Millers perform maintenance on the cottage themselves. If the Millers anticipate that depreciation will give them their main tax benefit, their personal use should not exceed the greater of 14 days per year or 10% of the rental period.

However, if interest, maintenance and real-estate taxes represent the significant part of total expenses, it might be better for them to use the property for more than 14 days. Then the cottage will be considered a second residence and the interest expense will be fully deductible.

What else should the Millers do?

A second strategy the Millers should consider is reducing their consumer debt. The tax deduction for consumer debt will be phased out over a five-year period. Beginning in 1987, 65% of consumer interest will be deductible; in 1988 40%; in 1989 20%, in 1990 10%; and none thereafter. By the way, interest paid to the IRS is considered consumer interest and is subject to the same limitations.

A final strategy is restructuring their investment portfolio from high-growth stocks to blue-chip stocks. Since the preferential treatment for long-term capital gains has been eliminated, high-growth stocks offering capital gain income may have lost some of their attractiveness. Blue-chip stocks which pay a good steady cash dividend have become more important.

Can Alan or Nancy work at home and deduct expenses?

Not recommended in their case, because the business part of the house must be the principal place of business, used exclusively for business. An additional requirement is that the business portion of the house must be for the convenience of the employer. And, household business deductions can only reduce business income, not create a tax loss. The Millers can also lose other future benefits by taking these deductions even if they qualify.

Is there any way the Millers can benefit from medical expense deductions?

Since 1983, medical expenses and medical insurance premiums have been deductible only to the extent that they exceeded 5% of adjusted gross income, rather than the 3% we have seen in the past. Beginning in 1987, that floor goes up to 7.5%. So, if the Millers' adjusted gross income is $60,000, for example, their medical expenses would have to be over $4,500 to yield any deductions.

Nancy's employment in a small boutique may provide her with an unusual opportunity normally not offered by larger companies. If a company sets up a medical expense reimbursement plan in a nondiscriminatory manner for its employees, then the company can reimburse the employees for medical payments that are not paid for by other insurance.

Those reimbursements would not be included as taxable income to the employees. Of course, an employee could not claim a deduction for the medical expenses in this case. This plan is a great fringe benefit in light of the increased tax floor on medical expense deductions.

How might medical reimbursements to Nancy affect Alan?

If Nancy can work out a plan with her employer, additional health insurance through Alan's company would probably be unnecessary. If Alan's company has a so-called "cafeteria plan" fringe benefit structure, Alan can decline the health insurance and take an equivalent benefit of some other kind, such as life insurance, retirement benefits or additional stock options.

How does the tax law affect Alan's stock options?

The difference between qualified and nonqualified stock options is no longer as significant as it was before the 1986 tax law. If it is qualified, the difference between the sales price and the purchase price may be treated as a capital gain, depending upon how long the stock is held.

In a nonqualified plan, a significant portion of the benefit will likely be taxed at ordinary income rates. Since capital gains will be taxed at the same rate as ordinary income, the advantage of qualified stock options is greatly diminished.

Investments

Are the Millers ready to begin an investment program?

Probably not yet. First, they don't have much liquidity, beyond $10,000 in a money market account. The rule-of-thumb here is that they ought to have about six months take-home pay in cash reserves. For the Millers, that amounts to $20,000.

Second, they have hefty cash needs in the near future. They recently acquired a summer cottage, and they will have the costs of mortgage, taxes, upkeep and so forth on that property. To exercise the stock options will require $25,000. And they will be paying college costs for six or seven years, beginning in two years when Frank is college age.

What should they do to improve their cash picture?

The Millers have about $5,000 available per year as discretionary income, after they pay for their basic needs. So they will have to work within that limit to figure out how some of their cash needs can be met.

They should increase their cash reserve until the account reaches a certain agreed-upon figure, say $20,000. To do this, the Millers should set aside each month a specific amount until that figure is reached.

Aren't the Millers' $10,000 in stocks liquid enough to be considered part of their cash reserves?

Not really. Common stocks are investments which can fluctuate in value. What if they had to withdraw funds in a period of depressed prices? To avoid this, they should use their money market account for their reserve.

They should look at the stocks they now own, cull out any under-performers, and reposition the portfolio to emphasize growth. If the Millers do this, they may find that a professionally managed mutual fund with a growth emphasis best suits their needs.

Do the Millers really need other stock investments, in addition to Alan's stock options?

The value of the options or the stock could be significantly affected by changes in the company, unanticipated changes in the tax law, or trends in the economy.

It is necessary to have some outside investments to counter any negative developments here.

Alan's stock options play an important role in the family's future, however. In order to tie the stock options in with a good overall financial plan, they should look at the terms of the options, the tax impact of the bargain element, the permissible timing of the exercise of the options, and the cash they will require to exercise the options. Then they can figure out how to take maximum advantage of the opportunity without disrupting the rest of their financial picture.

Are there tax-advantaged investments Alan and Nancy should consider?

They may wish to consider investing in single-premium variable life-insurance contracts or in tax-deferred annuities. In both instances, at present, earnings accumulate with no tax liabilities.

The success of an investment program depends on performance. However, the Millers could change their investments to adjust to different market or economic conditions. Unfortunately, as a result of changes made by the 1986 tax law, their combined incomes preclude tax-deductible contributions to IRAs.

Another asset that could provide some tax advantage is their summer cottage. Guidelines on the tax rules about rental property are discussed in the book section on tax planning.

What sort of overall investment plan should the Millers develop?

Basically, their investment plan can be divided into two parts. To begin with they should strive to maintain the status quo, that is, meet current expenses and plan for cash needs. They should exercise Alan's stock options and arrange for a maximum benefit from their summer cottage. They should also consider how best to use Nancy's anticipated inheritance for college expenses.

Once their children are through college, Alan and Nancy should emphasize asset accumulation for themselves with a mix of such traditional investments as stocks and bonds, and such non-traditional investments as limited partnerships and tax-favored insurance-company investment contracts.

Down the road, their combined incomes and the prospect that these incomes will increase requires them to make tax planning an integral part of their investment decision making.

Insurance

What insurance coverage do the Millers have?

Alan has a group life policy worth $100,000 through his employer. He also has a whole life policy of $50,000 of his own. Nancy has no life insurance. Alan's retirement plan is worth $60,000.

How much life insurance do the Millers need?

Alan will have a gross estate of approximately $275,000, not including any of the jointly held property. Most of the assets are liquid: $150,000 worth of life insurance, and retirement benefits of $60,000 which would be liquid at the time of his death.

With liquid assets of about $210,000 his family should be able to cover daily living expenses for a period immediately following Allen's death, and the estate will be able to pay federal and local estate taxes.

The family's needs over a more extended period are greater. Alan would like to provide an income for Nancy for her lifetime so that she can continue to enjoy her present lifestyle even after he dies. In addition to providing ordinary support for the kids, Alan would like to be able to provide for their college education.

Comparing the family's long-term needs with the liquid assets likely to be available on his death, it's clear that the $150,000 of life insurance Alan now has is not sufficient.

Why is Alan's life insurance not enough?

Start with $210,000 worth of liquid assets likely to be in Alan's estate. Based on the size of the estate, about $15,000 will be required to pay expenses related to funeral bills, medical bills, and the cost of administering the estate. Assume the state death taxes will take another $20,000 or so. Subtract that total of $35,000 from the $210,000 of liquid assets, and you're down to about $175,000.

That's a rough estimate of the money Nancy would have available to meet the family's needs. Assuming the funds are invested for an 8% yield, they would produce an income of $14,000 a year. That is the amount the family would have to live on, without consuming principal.

How much income will the family need?

Many of Alan and Nancy's expenses are fixed, such as the carrying costs of their real estate. A good rule of thumb is that Nancy would need somewhere around 70% of their combined income prior to Alan's death to maintain the family's lifestyle.

If their combined annual income is now $60,000, Nancy's need for cash will be about $42,000 a year. Nancy's own income is about $15,000 a year and her income from Alan's liquid assets will be approximately $14,000, a total of $29,000. Social security would pay about $500 a month, for an annual total of $6,000. This would leave Nancy about $8,000 short.

Alan therefore needs another $100,000 worth of life insurance to fund the $8,000 shortfall, and support Nancy and the children at their present standard of living.

How will college tuition be paid if Alan dies?

The Millers do not have enough life insurance now to pay for their children's college education without seriously reducing the income available to support the family's standard of living.

Alan could purchase a policy in an amount somewhat less than the anticipated cost of the college education. Then if he were to die, the proceeds of that policy could be invested, and the proceeds together with accumulated income earned would cover college costs. A policy in the amount of about $100,000 to $150,000 should suffice.

Should Nancy have life insurance?

What would the family's needs be if Nancy were to die before Alan? At present Nancy's job provides them with income to meet some of their essential expenses. Clearly, it would be necessary to provide Alan with replacement income upon Nancy's death.

Also, since Nancy performs many household and family tasks which Alan would not have adequate time to do, Alan would have to hire a housekeeper. Assume it would cost Alan an additional $10,000 a year to pay someone to perform those household chores.

Nancy's income is then actually $25,000: $15,000 for the part-time job and $10,000 worth of household services.

Although the need for daily living expenses may decrease somewhat as the children get older, the need for educational expenses will increase.

How much insurance should Nancy have?

A $50,000 policy on Nancy's life is recommended, with a double-indemnity rider so that if she died by accident, it would pay $100,000. The income and principal from the insurance could be used by Alan to satisfy cash requirements over the next several years. He should probably plan to spend the principal, expecting that about five years following Nancy's death his income alone will cover the family's needs.

Another aspect of Nancy's insurance needs is death taxes, both state and federal. While the Miller's assets will likely avoid federal estate taxes on the death of one spouse, the death of the surviving spouse may mean substantial federal estate taxes. Given the size of the Miller's estates at this time, the insurance suggested should provide enough cash to meet the tax burden.

Is it safe to rely on Alan's group life insurance?

Given the fact that Alan is young and is in good graces with the company, it makes sense to plan on that insurance for the next three to five years. However, if Alan takes a new job with a different company, he must make sure that his new company provides similar benefits.

He should also be concerned about his retirement benefit if he changed jobs. The value of his retirement benefit is $60,000. Unless that benefit is vested, Alan might lose a portion of it if he changed jobs.

What type of insurance should the Millers have?

A combination of permanent and term insurance is recommended for the Millers because their living expenses just about consume their income. $50,000 of the additional insurance recommended should be permanent and the balance in term insurance. This will keep the cost down, and as their income increases they can convert the term insurance to permanent coverage without submitting a health statement.

Another advantage to permanent coverage, in addition to being a better value, is the loan value of the policy. This may be important to Alan when his children are of college age. He can borrow money against the policy at a low interest rate to pay college tuition.

Who should own these policies?

Alan could own the insurance on Alan's life, Nancy could own it, or an irrevocable trust could own it. Nancy should own the policy on her life while it is a relatively small amount. If Alan owns the policy on his life and dies, the face amount of the policy will be included in his estate for tax purposes. If Nancy or an irrevocable trust owns the policy, the proceeds will probably not be included in his estate. Based on the size of Alan's estate at this time, it is not necessary to create an irrevocable insurance trust.

If the size of Alan's or Nancy's estate increases substantially in the future, it may be to their advantage to set up an irrevocable trust and assign the ownership of both his group term insurance and his whole life insurance to the trust. That way, life-insurance proceeds will probably escape taxation at his death. Furthermore, those insurance proceeds may avoid taxation in Nancy's estate as well. Simply assigning the policies to Nancy will avoid taxation in Alan's estate but, if Nancy still has any of the proceeds when she dies, they will be taxed in her estate.

Who should be the beneficiaries of the respective insurance policies?

As it stands now, the Millers have not set up living trusts, but if they create such trusts, they should certainly consider the trust as a beneficiary. Until then, each should be the other's primary beneficiary.

Estate Planning

What estate planning objectives should the Millers have?

Alan and Nancy will want to maximize their spendable income over the next few years. They are also interested in the tax consequences of gifts, because Nancy's father wants to give the Miller children, Frank and Martha, some money.

Their primary objectives, however, should be to conserve estate assets by minimizing taxes, and providing as much continuity as possible in the event either should die. They should therefore plan to make wills.

They also should plan on distributing property through trusts in order to minimize transfer costs, which include estate taxes, probate costs and legal fees.

Is there anything else the Millers should do?

Alan and Nancy should execute powers of attorney, legal documents which allow each to bind the other in legal transactions. This power can be revoked at any time, and it can be useful if either becomes mentally or physically ill or goes away on extensive travel.

What would their wills do?

The wills would be relatively simple documents which direct the assets into trusts. In addition, the wills might direct tangibles to the surviving spouse or to the children, and they would contain other specific bequests Alan or Nancy wished to include. One of the most important functions of the wills would be the appointment of guardians and executors.

Nancy's mother died several months ago, leaving essentially everything to Nancy's father. Is there anything he can do to prevent this from increasing the likely tax burden on his estate?

If Nancy's father disclaims his share of his wife's estate, that share is treated just as if he had predeceased his wife. In this case, the will directs the assets to go then to Nancy, her brother and her sister. A disclaimer thus would keep those assets from passing through Nancy's father's estate, saving on taxes and expenses. In a sense, it rewrites the mother's will.

111

There is something else the beneficiaries should know. If the estate does not have to pay federal estate taxes, then the estate can pass the deductibility of its administration expenses to the beneficiaries, to be reported on their personal income-tax returns in proportion to their shares of the estate. It's a small point, but it can save money.

Are there other issues of estate planning for Alan and Nancy to consider?

Yes. Nancy and Alan presently own both their home and the summer cottage jointly, which could reduce probate costs. However, greater savings could be realized if the property were owned individually and directed into a trust upon the death of the owner. The property would then not be included in the surviving spouse's estate, thus reducing estate taxes.

Since real estate makes up the bulk of their present net worth, they probably should take advantage of the greater estate-planning flexibility they would have if the property were owned individually.

Would a transfer of the real-estate property be difficult to accomplish?

No. The process is straightforward. Alan and Nancy simply execute a deed conveying property to one or the other individually. It would be essential first to tell the banks holding the mortgages. The Millers would not wish inadvertently to give the banks a right to call a loan or to raise the interest rate.

Is it really all that simple?

There are other considerations. Owning the houses together gives them each some control over the property, which they may prefer for the time being. Also, if their marriage got into trouble, individual ownership might lead to a dispute during distribution of the property in a divorce.

If the Millers decide on individual ownership, should they transfer both pieces of real estate to Nancy, in order to equalize estates?

That would certainly make sense for estate planning purposes, because Nancy's holdings are a lot less than Alan's. Nancy would own the houses in a trust, and her trust should contain a provision that the houses be used for Alan's benefit during his life.

Nancy may inherit property from her parents. Does that make the real-estate transfer unnecessary?

An inheritance by Nancy could equalize their holdings somewhat, but right now, Alan owns $250,000 more than Nancy. Unless she inherits a sizable amount soon, the transfer of real estate to her may still be the best route.

Why is it so important to have the estates the same size?

There are really two reasons. First, the estate tax is graduated. There will be less in total taxes on Nancy's and Alan's estates as a whole, because they will both be on a lower part of the graduated tax scale, than if one is taxed in the higher ranges and the other not at all.

The second reason is to fully use the unified credit. As mentioned, $600,000 of property can pass free of federal tax because of the unified credit. It would be a partial waste of that credit to have one estate exceed the amount and the other be substantially under.

If both houses were put in Nancy's name and Alan died, he would leave an estate of about $275,000; or nearer $475,000 if he buys additional life insurance.

The houses are worth $95,000, plus $10,000 for Nancy's tangibles, and another $50,000 if she buys life insurance. That puts her estate up to about $150,000, not counting any potential inheritance.

So the Millers, with potential combined estates in the $600,000 range, need not be overly concerned for now. But it's something for them to keep in mind as their assets increase over the years.

How often should the Millers revise their estate plan to make sure it is still suitable?

Barring any unusual changes, they should check on it every three to five years to make sure it accomplishes their goals. There are certain changes that could trigger an immediate review of the plan.

Sudden substantial increases in income or net worth would warrant a review of the plan, as would death or divorce. If Alan and Nancy are considering buying real estate or other property of significant value, they should have some advice on how title should be taken; that is, who should own it.

And if the Millers change their principal residence to a different state, their wills and trusts should be analyzed to see how they operate under the laws of that new state. Finally, changes in the estate tax laws would certainly call for a review of the Miller's documents.

Gifts

How would gifts from Nancy's father affect their planning?

Nancy's father can give any one person up to $10,000 per year with no federal gift tax, and he can do this for as many people as he likes. If he wanted to give the Miller family as much money as possible, he can give Nancy, Alan, Martha and Frank each $10,000 per year for a total of $40,000, free of gift tax.

He can give an unlimited amount with no gift tax, if the funds are paid directly to an educational institution for tuition costs for his grandchildren. Depending on his resources, Nancy's father could prove to be a big help with the college tuition bills.

If the gifts to Alan or Nancy exceed $10,000 in any one year, the gift tax on the amount in excess of $10,000 could be offset by the unified credit until that credit is used up.

Would a gifting program also help Nancy's father reduce potential estate taxes?

Hard to say without knowing more about his assets and what he is inheriting from his wife. But there are things he should be thinking about in doing his own estate planning.

He ought to have a durable power of attorney so that someone can manage his affairs if he becomes incapacitated. He should make sure his will is current.

He may want to create a grantor trust such as we have described for Alan and Nancy and put assets in the trust for his own benefit. Or he may decide to create a family trust where the trustees have broad power to pay income and distribute principal among a number of family members according to their needs.

Nancy or her brother or sister may be the appropriate beneficiaries now, but the trustees would probably begin making payments directly to the grandchildren at some point in the future. Also, if Nancy's father has his assets in a trust, then the family may realize substantial savings on estate administration.

What if Nancy's father does not want to give large sums of money outright to Frank and Martha, considering that they are only sixteen and fourteen?

He can create a trust for the benefit of his grandchildren and then make transfers to the trust. There are various forms of trusts which can be used for this purpose. Or he can make gifts under the Uniform Gifts to Minors Act or the Uniform Transfer to Minors Act.

Trusts

What kind of trust should the Millers use?

Nancy and Alan should each consider setting up a revocable living grantor trust. They should also balance their estates by conveying assets to Nancy. The trusts would then "mirror" one another.

Alan would appoint himself as trustee of his trust during his life or for as long as he was capable of being trustee. The trust instrument would provide for a successor trustee. Nancy and her trust would do the same.

As an alternative, if Nancy's net worth stays at about where it is now, she would not need a trust. She could have a simple will which would distribute her property to Alan.

If Alan dies first, her will would put her property into Alan's trust, to be held for the benefit of the children rather than given to them outright.

Will it cost the Millers a lot of money to create a trust?

The cost of drafting a trust document is relatively modest, unless they ask for some especially fancy provisions.

A trust becomes functional when it is funded. They can fund a trust with only one dollar for now, just to bring it into existence.

Nancy and Alan would make wills directing their estate assets into their trusts. The trust instruments would govern the distribution of those assets.

When should a trust be more fully funded?

It might be desirable for Nancy's assets to be conveyed to her trust now if, for example, she were to become disabled or if she wanted to be relieved of financial management responsibilities at some point in her life. The successor trustees would take over management.

Life-insurance proceeds should be payable to the trusts, particularly where insurance represents the bulk of the estate, assuming that the trust will hold assets for the benefit of the rest of the family. Then, for example, if Alan dies, the proceeds of his policy would be paid to his grantor trust to be used in accordance with the terms of the trust.

If Alan purchased additional life insurance with the specific aim of providing for his children's education, he may want to include some language in the trust instrument directing the trustees to use the funds for that purpose.

What benefits can Alan and Nancy anticipate from trusts?

A trust can provide flexibility in the distribution of assets over a period of years. Another primary aim is tax savings. When the first spouse dies, say Alan, his assets can pass free of federal estate tax to Nancy because of the unlimited marital deduction.

When Nancy dies, her estate could be subject to substantial federal estate tax, assuming it is greater than the amount excused by the unified credit provision. Called the exemption equivalent, this allows $600,000 to pass free of federal estate taxes.

Alan's trust can help Nancy's estate avoid being taxed on an amount of property equal to the exemption equivalent. Then Alan's assets can pass directly to the children after her death. But during her life, the trustees of Alan's trust will hold the assets for her benefit. The trust can also save some probate costs associated with the second estate.

I should mention that any joint property will automatically pass to the surviving joint tenant so it will not become part of the trust assets.

I'm really getting confused now. Can you give me some specifics?

Here is how a trust for Alan might be structured. First, we add up the value of property Alan holds in his own name, separate from the property held jointly with Nancy. He has $150,000 of life insurance. We'll assume he has added another $150,000 of insurance on our recommendation. His retirement plan is worth $60,000, and his stock options are worth $50,000 (net value). Adding tangibles, the total at present comes to $425,000, but our planning should assume that it will be greater at Alan's death.

The trust would segregate the estate assets into two categories at the time of his death. One category is the "credit shelter" or "family share." It would contain an amount equal to the exemption equivalent, the amount ($600,000) that can pass free of federal estate tax because of the unified credit.

The other category is the "marital deduction share," which would contain any amount in excess of $600,000. No tax would be paid on that because it would qualify for the marital deduction. To have it qualify, the trust provisions must give Nancy at least the right to the income from the assets for as long as she lives.

What happens to the "credit shelter" part?

During Nancy's life, Alan's trust holds these assets for her benefit and the children's benefit. The trustees might be given authority to pay income and distribute principal among Nancy, the children, and any grandchildren.

On Nancy's death the assets can be directed to the children outright or continue to be held in trust, according to whatever provisions Alan selects. They won't be taxed in Nancy's estate because she did not have control.

Will this setup work in any state?

The death tax laws of the different states vary widely and sometimes the taxes of the states can impose a much greater burden than the federal laws, because the unified credit and unlimited federal marital deduction may eliminate the federal tax altogether.

What should the Millers do about the choice of fiduciaries?

For now, Alan and Nancy will each be trustee of his or her own grantor trust. It should be fairly easy to manage assets of $1.00, especially when you are your own beneficiary, but on the other hand, the job doesn't pay much, either.

The question really is who to appoint as standby trustees to serve when the Millers no longer can. Two co-trustees are recommended, a family member and an independent trustee such as an attorney or bank trust officer.

The family member supplies the personal input. The independent, professional trustee is helpful in achieving a separation of beneficiaries from control over the property so that the trust will operate as an estate tax shelter.

If you have only a family member who is a trustee and also a beneficiary of the trust, that person may be considered to control the property for his own use. When that beneficiary dies, the trust assets may be included in his estate for tax purposes, which defeats the estate tax-sheltering goals.

What else should Nancy and Alan keep in mind in choosing executors and guardians?

One of the major functions of a will is to nominate executors and guardians. They would do well to appoint each other as executor or executrix if they both are competent in business matters.

They should consider appointing a professional as co-executor or at least be prepared to obtain sufficient professional assistance in administering the estate. They also must name alternates.

The executors will collect the assets of the estate, file the necessary papers with the probate court, pay estate taxes, and deliver property to the trustees of the trusts or the named beneficiaries.

The choice of guardians for their minor children has even more far-reaching consequences. They will want someone who loves the children and can offer them a good environment. Perhaps they will consider another married couple with children of similar age, such as one of Nancy's siblings.

And a guardian should have sufficient funds to support the children, which will be the case if the estate-planning and life-insurance recommendations are followed.

This concludes the Miller family case study.

Case Study:
High-Income
Family

Introduction

This case study focuses on the Huntingtons, a hypothetical family with an income of $100,000 per year. The purpose of the study is to illustrate how professional advisors would develop a financial plan for such a family, to prepare you to ask the right questions during an initial financial planning meeting, and to give you enough background to evaluate the answers.

What is the Huntington's income picture?

Dick and Susan Huntington are both in their late 40s. Dick is a vice president in a large international company and earns over $100,000 a year. His prospects, as they say, are good. Susan has a modest income from securities.

What assets do they have?

Dick holds cash and marketable securities worth about $450,000. Susan has about $50,000 in cash and securities. The equity in their home (net after deducting the mortgage) is about $275,000. They have about $200,000 equity in a summer home. They own both houses jointly. Their tangible personal property, including automobiles, antiques, jewelry, and so on, come to about $25,000 for Dick and about $40,000 for Susan.

What is their insurance coverage?

Dick has a group life insurance policy worth $200,000 and a whole life policy for $50,000. Susan has $10,000 of life insurance. Dick also has a $100,000 pension plan.

What is their total worth?

Dick's property comes to $825,000, while Susan's is $100,000. Those figures include the cash and securities, tangibles and insurance. The real estate totals $475,000.

The Huntington's assets are summarized in the accompanying chart.

Summary of Assets Of Dick and Susan Huntington

	Dick's Property	Susan's Property	Joint Property
Home (net of mortgage)			$ 275,000
Summer Home (net of mortgage)			$ 200,000
Marketable Securities	$450,000	$ 50,000	
Tangible Personal Property	$ 25,000	$ 40,000	
Group Life Insurance	$200,000		
Whole Life Policy	$ 50,000	$ 10,000	
Retirement plan	$100,000		
Totals	$825,000	$100,000	$ 475,000
Potential inheritance	$500,000		
Combined total			$1,900,000

What is their family situation?

Dick's father is deceased. His mother has about $500,000 worth of assets. Dick has no brothers or sisters. Susan's mother is deceased. Her father has few assets and may need financial assistance from Dick and Susan. Dick's mother and Susan's father are both well along in years.

Dick and Susan have two grown children. Their son, Eric, is in his second marriage. He has two children by his first marriage and one by his second. Eric has a semi-skilled job and has trouble making ends meet.

Their daughter, Sally, is not married and has no immediate plans to marry. She has a good career as a surgeon and earns a high income.

Tax Planning

Last year, the Huntingtons paid a very high percentage of their income in taxes. They had significant income from sources other than wages: capital gains, dividends and bonuses which occurred late in the year. The objective here is to reduce the tax as much as possible, consistent with Dick and Susan's liquidity needs.

Can they use gifts to reduce their income taxes?

The transfer of gifts has no direct effect on income taxes, although the income from a gift could, if the recipient is under age fourteen. Dick and Susan can each transfer $10,000 per year to as many individuals as they want without paying any gift tax.

If the amount of a gift exceeds $10,000 for a year, they can still apply it to the unified credit and avoid current payment of gift taxes. They should understand, though, that this uses up some of the unified credit, cutting down the amount that can be used to reduce estate taxes later on.

What can the Huntingtons do to minimize their tax burden?

As a general rule, as the end of the year approaches, Dick and Susan may want to accelerate deductions for state taxes by prepaying some of their state taxes before December 31. They may be able to do this with some of their real-estate taxes as well. They should probably also look at ways of deferring and excluding income.

Investing in certificates of deposit or U.S. Treasury bills which mature after year-end defers income to the following year. Another way they could exclude income from taxation is by purchasing tax-exempt bonds.

Suppose they invested in rental property. Can they defer rental income?

Most tenants would not object to a delay in rental payments. However, a concept called the "constructive receipt doctrine" might be used by the IRS to hold that, even if they did not actually receive the rental income, it was available to them, so they should include it. Keep in mind also that rental property is now considered a passive income activity under the 1986 tax law.

How would the passive classification affect rental deductions for Dick and Susan?

In simple terms it means that many taxpayers will no longer be able to use net losses arising from investments in limited partnerships, tax shelters or any other activity where the taxpayer does not participate.

By definition, real-estate rental activity is now considered passive. However, losses up to $25,000 from such rental activities will be allowed if a taxpayer actively participates in managing it and has an annual adjusted gross income of $100,000 or less. For every dollar over $100,000, the $25,000 loss must be reduced by 50 cents. So, if Dick made an income of $150,000, he would not be allowed a rental deduction.

If the Huntingtons bought a two-family apartment building that generated a loss of $10,000, would they be able to deduct it?

Some of it, if they actively managed the unit, and their adjusted gross income did not exceed $150,000. Also, under the phase-in rule, they will be able to deduct 65% of the disallowable portion of any losses in 1987, 40% in 1988, 20% in 1989, 10% in 1990, but none in the year thereafter.

If they do not actively manage the rental unit, the $25,000 loss limitation does not apply, but the phase-in rule does apply. Any non-deductible rental losses could be carried over to future years to offset net income from the rental or sale of the property.

What if the Huntingtons own a vacation property in the mountains that they rent out. Will they still be able to deduct a loss on it?

If the property is actively managed by them, the same rules apply. However, if the property is a seasonal home which they do not rent, they may deduct the interest and taxes paid on it.

Would it be worthwhile for Dick and Susan to refinance their home to free up additional cash for gifts, trusts and investments?

Yes, if they do not borrow more than an amount not exceeding the original cost of the house plus any improvements made, so that they can deduct the loan interest. If they borrow for either medical or educational purposes, they can borrow up to the fair market value of the house and deduct the interest.

Can Susan sell stock to her son Eric for some small amount, and let him sell it later to pay for his children's college educations?

To constitute a true sale, the transaction must be for fair market value. Otherwise, the IRS might view the transaction as part sale and part gift, which could result in income and gift tax consequences.

Moreover, if the stock were given outright and sold immediately, the giver could still be taxed on the entire capital gain. The only purpose of the gift, the IRS could argue, was to transfer parental income to Eric. If Eric held the stock for a reasonable period and then sold it, the gain would be taxable on his return.

If Dick gets a new car, should he or his business buy it?

If he uses the car mostly for business travel, it is probably better to buy it through his business. Interest payments on car loans will be deductible by a business after 1986, but will be subject to limitations if deducted by an individual.

If Dick and Susan pay for the cost of a babysitter for Eric's youngest child, can they take advantage of the child-care tax credit?

No, because the child doesn't live in their household and is not claimed as a dependent on their return.

Will the alternative minimum tax have any effect on the Huntingtons?

The alternative minimum tax (AMT) may have some unexpected applications that could throw a monkey wrench in their tax planning. It could be triggered by so-called preference items in their investment program, for example.

Congress was concerned that certain taxpayers with significant deductions, such as net losses from passive income activities and tax-exempt interest on non-governmental bonds, were not paying their fair share of taxes. As a result, the AMT was devised.

If the Huntingtons have a significant tax benefit from these and other preference items, then they must compute both the regular income tax and the AMT, and pay the higher figure. If there's no way of avoiding the AMT in this sort of situation, the best bet is to accelerate income and postpone deductions. For example, Dick could take an advance on his salary.

Are there any other tax saving devices Dick and Susan can use?

There are several things in the nature of fringe benefits Dick could discuss with his company. A qualified retirement program such as a pension or profit-sharing plan would provide an excellent opportunity for tax-free appreciation. He already has a pension plan, but he might want to look into adding to it. In a large corporate pension plan today $100,000 is not an unusually large amount.

He should also ask whether his employer has considered a health insurance plan. Premiums and reimbursements paid by the business would not be taxable to Dick or Susan. A medical reimbursement plan which covers those items not covered by regular health insurance can provide a significant benefit. This type of plan must be applied on a non-discriminatory basis, however.

Is there anything Dick and Susan should do before the end of this year to obtain tax savings before April 15 of next year?

They can probably improve their cash flow almost immediately. Dick should review his withholding for the year. Since his taxable income will be less, he may be able to reduce his withholding by amending his W-4. Likewise, if he has made estimated tax payments (because of his unearned income), he should review these as well, since the final payment may be unnecessary.

Investments

The Huntingtons have substantial investments. Are there other ideas they should consider for their investment portfolio?

Dick's basic salary level is at $100,000, but over the last several years he has received bonuses, interest, and dividends which have brought his income into the $150,000 range.

Their main objective should be to minimize taxes on their investments, in an effort to maximize the accumulation of assets toward Dick's retirement.

What approach is recommended?

A program should be designed which focuses on two objectives: reduce taxable income from investments to a minimum, and produce whatever tax benefits are available under the 1986 tax law to reduce the tax on earned income. The 1986 tax law severely restricts the ability to offset against income large tax deductions from investments, but it does allow some benefits through specialized investing.

What types of investments are suggested?

First, Dick and Susan need to have investments independent from Dick's employer, to protect against having too much in one security, and to balance against adverse developments that might occur in the future.

Beyond this, there are tax-advantaged investments that can help reduce taxes, such as (1) tax-exempt bonds for the conservative part of the portfolio because income earned from them is free from federal and state taxes, and (2) tax-deferred variable annuities and investment life-insurance contracts, offering the tax shelter of growth with the opportunity to invest in managed stock portfolios, thus combining tax benefits with investments.

Are there any other investments they should consider?

Investment real estate, done either individually or through a limited partnership, is certainly worthy of their consideration. The combination of these ideas will allow Dick and Susan to participate in growth and compounding without taxes along the way.

How can real-estate investment reduce tax on earned income?

Dick and Susan can make investments in programs which offer investment tax credits, such as low-income housing and rehabilitation of older buildings. These credits directly reduce income taxes owed.

The use of these credits is not unlimited. Up to $25,000 of income can be sheltered from tax, provided that Dick's income does not exceed $200,000. In addition, the credits are available for property acquired only until 1990 for low-income housing and until 1994 for rehabilitation.

Should Dick and Susan's real-estate investments be limited to these two opportunities?

Not necessarily. Other types of real-estate, such as apartment buildings, offices, warehouses or shopping centers can provide long-term appreciation, and along the way, throw off tax deductions which can shelter from tax any income that they or other like-kind investments produce.

What part of the Huntington portfolio should be devoted to real estate?

Real estate does not have ready liquidity. Dick and Susan should not commit so much that they compromise their ability to raise cash. Real estate is an investment like any other, and should be part of but not the whole of an investment portfolio. The Huntington's commitment to real estate should reflect how they feel about it and how it best fits into their planning for the future.

Insurance

An overall financial plan for the entire Huntington family should accommodate the insurance needs of each member of the family, including Dick and Susan, their parents, and their children and grandchildren.

Those needs should be viewed in the light of the availability of cash, or other "liquid" assets which can easily be converted to cash to provide for immediate needs if a family member dies.

If there is a need for insurance, the plan should reflect the types of insurance best for each person. Finally, the plan should designate for each policy who should be the owner and who should be the beneficiary.

Who's on first?

Because he is the principal breadwinner, Dick is the keystone of the plan. Dick's assets would produce a gross estate of approximately $825,000, not including any of the jointly held property. Most of that is liquid.

The $450,000 in cash and marketable securities is liquid. The $250,000 worth of life insurance is liquid. His pension-plan benefits of $100,000 would be liquid at the time of his death. So his liquid assets come to about $800,000, which is adequate liquidity in the estate at this time.

Does Dick need insurance?

Dick would like to provide an income for Susan for her lifetime so that she can continue to enjoy her present lifestyle even after he dies. His mother probably does not need any assistance; she has $500,000 of her own. He may want to provide for Susan's father. We can assume that Dick's daughter, like his son, may have some need for support and assistance.

Comparing his family's needs with the liquid assets likely to be available on his death, the $250,000 in life insurance Dick now has offers sufficient coverage.

Is it safe to bank on the fact that $200,000 is group life insurance, since that depends on Dick remaining in his job?

Given the fact that Dick is in his 40s and is in good graces with the company, It should be safe to plan on that insurance for the next three to five years. However, the group coverage will cease at his retirement, and it would be very expensive for him to purchase other life insurance at that time.

Dick should be encouraged to negotiate with his company for some form of life-insurance coverage that would protect him after he retires. Life insurance companies are now introducing a number of plans that will provide continued coverage beyond retirement.

With liquid assets of about $800,000, would Dick's estate be adequate to provide for Susan's needs?

A good rule of thumb is that Susan would need 50% to 70% of Dick's income prior to his death in order to maintain her lifestyle. If Dick were making $100,00 a year, Susan's need for cash would be $50,00 to $70,000 a year.

Subtract from the $800,000 liquidity in Dick's estate approximately $40,000 to pay expenses and bills related to administering the estate. Then subtract another $60,000 for estimated state death taxes.

Invested at 8%, the remaining $700,000 would produce an income of about $60,000 per year. That is the amount Susan would have to live on without consuming principal, and it fits into the rule-of-thumb estimate of her needs.

What are Susan's life insurance needs?

Susan already has $10,000 worth of life insurance. If the Huntingtons transfer some of Dick's assets to Susan and also shift to her the jointly held property, Susan's estate would include the $275,000 principal home and the $200,000 summer home, together with perhaps another $200,000 or $300,000 of liquid assets transferred to her from Dick's portfolio.

If Susan were to die before Dick, she would therefore have an estate of about $700,000. Adding the $50,000 worth of cash in her own name, plus $40,000 worth of tangible personal property such as jewelry, her gross estate would be roughly $800,000.

The debts and expenses of administering that estate computed at 5% would be approximately $40,000. Adding an estimated $60,000 to pay state death taxes, $100,000 might be required to clear her estate.

At present, her liquid assets are sufficient to cover that cash flow, and she does not need additional insurance. However, using the liquidity to clear the estate does mean a reduction in the amount passing to her beneficiaries at the time of her death.

Dick and Susan must decide whether they want to cover that reduction with additional insurance on Susan.

What life-insurance coverage should the other members of the family have?

Dick's mother does not need insurance. Susan's father, although he needs some cash, does not need insurance. Neither parent has dependents to provide for at this point, both of the elderly people would be difficult to insure, and the insurance would be very expensive.

Dick and Susan's daughter, Sally, is healthy and does not have anyone at present who depends upon her income. Nevertheless, she would be wise to buy a policy now to establish the premium rate while she is still young and healthy. If she marries and has a family, she will have already established a good base for her future estate planning.

Their son Eric has three children and a fairly modest income. Life insurance could be very important to his family. Dick and Susan should consider covering the premium payments for Eric so that he can establish a well-organized insurance plan for his family.

Dick could also buy life-insurance policies for his grandchildren. At their young ages, the premiums would be very low. Starting the policies now would be a big benefit to them later on.

Which type of policies should the Huntingtons have?

There are really two basic types of life insurance policies available: term insurance and permanent insurance, along with a number of variations of each. Permanent insurance is recommended for the Huntingtons. Dick and Susan have enough cash coming in to pay the premiums.

If the Huntington's son, Eric, buys his own insurance, he may only have enough cash to purchase a term policy. The fact that Dick could provide permanent insurance for Eric is a real planning opportunity.

Furthermore, the loan value of a permanent policy may be of great importance to Eric when his children get to be of college age. He can borrow money against the policy at a low interest rate to pay college costs—knowing, of course, that such interest is not deductible on an individual tax return.

Would split-dollar insurance be a good idea?

Split-dollar life insurance is an arrangement whereby Dick could obtain additional life insurance at a very low cost. Dick's company would take out a policy on Dick's life and pay the premium. At the time of Dick's death, the employer would be repaid from the proceeds, and the balance would go to Dick's beneficiaries.

This may be a particularly good idea if the Huntingtons shift some of Dick's liquid assets to their children, or if Dick is concerned about losing his group insurance when he retires. In any case, it provides a little more coverage if Susan needed somewhat more than $60,000 per year.

If Dick, Susan, and Eric are insured, who should own the policies?

Dick could own his, Susan could own both, or an irrevocable trust could own them. If Dick owns his policy and dies, the face amount would be included in his estate. If Susan or an irrevocable trust owned the policy, the proceeds would probably not be included in his estate, and thus escape taxation on his estate.

To avoid taxation in Susan's estate as well, Dick should create such a trust, and assign the ownership of both his group term insurance and his $50,000 whole life insurance to it. If Dick assigned those policies to Susan, it is likely that the policies would be included in her estate.

Susan could own the policy on her own life as long as it is for a relatively small amount. Another irrevocable trust could be created for insurance on Eric for the benefit of his family, so that the proceeds are not included in Eric's estate.

Who should be the beneficiaries of the various insurance policies?

If Dick creates an irrevocable life-insurance trust, the trust itself should be both the owner and beneficiary of the policy. This will serve to provide maximum benefits from the policy itself, and at the same time transfer the proceeds out of Dick's taxable estate.

If it is not desirable to create such a trust, Dick and Susan may each buy policies on the other's life, with the owner of the policy also the beneficiary. This excludes the benefits from the decedent's taxable estate.

Assuming the Huntingtons elect to create living trusts, it is wise to designate those trusts as beneficiaries. The life-insurance proceeds can then be allocated within the revocable trust to fund a credit shelter (or bypass) trust to protect up to $600,000 from taxation on the death of the second spouse.

Estate Planning

What advice should the Huntington family follow on estate planning?

It's safe to assume the Huntingtons want to pass on as much property as possible to their children and their grandchildren, provided that they can continue to maintain their present lifestyle.

As part of their estate plan, they should provide for that distribution by using wills, trusts, and gifts. At the same time, they want to save transfer costs, which include the cost of probate, legal fees, gift tax expenses and estate tax costs.

Also, they want to try to reduce income taxes by shifting income and capital appreciation from family members in high tax brackets to other members in lower tax brackets.

How should Dick and Susan take care of themselves?

Dick and Susan appear able to support their own lifestyle. Beyond protecting their present situation, they need not increase their present assets significantly. That would simply increase estate-tax costs in the future. Instead, they should consider gifting programs for their children and their grandchildren.

Protecting their present situation means they want to maintain their standard of living while they are both alive, and preserve that standard of living for the surviving spouse if one of them dies. And they want to preserve as much continuity as possible in their business affairs.

What is their first step?

During their lifetime, they should both execute powers of attorney. Those are simple legal documents which would allow Susan, for instance, to undertake any legal transactions for Dick. She could then sign a contract, endorse stock certificates or enter into other arrangements binding upon Dick, in Dick's extended absence or disability.

How will the Huntington's estate plan save probate costs?

Remember that probate assets are assets which a person owns individually at the time of his or her death. Assume that Susan dies before Dick. Any assets which she owns individually would be subjected to the expenses of probating her estate: probate court fees, legal fees and executor's fees.

If Susan during her lifetime has transferred some of her assets to her trust, those assets are not owned individually by her, but are assets of her trust. Since they are not probate assets, they would not incur probate expenses.

These expenses vary in proportion to the amount of the assets going through probate. Reducing probate assets can save some probate costs.

How much are the expenses of probate?

Planners generally use 5% of the value of the assets as an estimate of the costs of the last illness and the expenses required to administer the estate. (There may be additional costs related to administering property, such as appraisal costs and the expense of preparing income and estate tax returns.)

The expenses of administering non-probate assets are estimated at one half the expense of administering probate assets. The percentage of probate expenses decreases as the value of the estate increases. So the saving from having property in trust might be 2% or more of the value of estate assets that do not go through probate.

Can the Huntingtons do anything as part of their estate planning to minimize executor's fees and legal fees?

If they select a family member to serve as executor, that person may decide to waive the fees. No special method exists for reducing legal fees, although the executor has a responsibility to make sure that the charges are reasonable.

Do the Huntingtons need advice on estate and trust administration?

Not in the strict sense, because they don't have an estate or a trust to administer. However, there are some estate-planning considerations for Dick's mother and Susan's father.

There should also be some estate planning done for the Huntington children. Then there are issues raised by jointly held property. Next are the Huntingtons' choice of fiduciaries, that is, executors and trustees.

Finally, there are the various types of trusts recommended to the Huntingtons. When should they put funds in these trusts? How will the trusts actually operate?

What estate plan is envisioned for Dick and Susan's parents?

Dick's mother and Susan's father should each give powers of attorney to Dick and Susan, so that Susan will have authority to act for her father and Dick can act for his mother. If state law permits, both should be durable powers, so they'll continue to be valid if the person granting the power becomes incapacitated.

Also, both parents should have up-to-date wills. Even though Susan's father does not have a large estate, it will be easier to administer if his will is current. That way, there's no guesswork about who should receive his property or who he wants as executor.

He may want to leave his tangible personal property to Susan and any other assets to the children, so that the other property would not be taxed in Susan's estate.

Should the Huntingtons own property jointly or individually?

As a general rule, estate planners advise clients to own property individually. The Huntingtons could transfer jointly owned property to one spouse or the other. In these circumstances, it makes sense to increase the size of Susan's estate to roughly equal to Dick's estate. One good way to do that is to transfer both jointly owned houses to her.

Dick and Susan as joint tenants would sign a deed for the property to Susan, first notifying the banks that hold the mortgages. Otherwise, the bank might exercise its right to call a loan which has a low interest rate. Dick and Susan will want to hold onto those low interest-rate mortgages for as long as they can.

There is another delicate issue. With a divorce rate of almost 50%, people should be careful about dividing property. Before dividing jointly held property, a couple must be certain they are each satisfied that the marriage is strong. It might change their negotiating positions if they found themselves embroiled in divorce proceedings after the transfer.

Why should Susan and Dick have estates of equal size?

Two reasons, basically. One is that the estate-tax rates are graduated. There will be less in total taxes if both estates are taxed in a lower range of the graduated estate tax, than if one estate is taxed in the upper range and the other estate taxed not at all.

The second reason is that, under the unified credit provision, the amount of property which can pass free of taxation is $600,000. To take maximum advantage of that law, both estates must have assets which total at least that amount.

Since the Huntingtons' total gross assets amount to about $1.4 million, it's possible to balance their assets so that both Susan and Dick each have an estate of about $700,000.

Wills

If property management is going to be done through trusts, the wills are fairly simple, right?

True, but do not overlook other functions of a will. One is to name executors to collect the assets of the estate, file the necessary papers with the probate court, pay estate taxes, and deliver property to the trustees of the trusts. Another is to name guardians to care for minors or incompetents.

What about a will for Dick's mother?

Her situation is a little more complicated since she has about $500,000 worth of property. Dick's mother's will should pass her tangible personal property to Dick, and the rest of her property into a family trust.

If it is held in trust for the benefit of Dick and Susan's children and grandchildren, it will not be included in Dick or Susan's estates. This generation-skipping will save both estate taxes and administration expenses. Because the amount is below $1 million, there is no need to worry about the generation-skipping transfer tax.

Another possibility is that Dick's mother create a grantor trust to hold all her property for her benefit during her life. This would be useful if she wanted help in managing the money later on. At the time of her death, the property could pass outside the probate process to Dick and his children or to other beneficiaries.

What about wills for the Huntington children, Eric and Sally?

If Dick and Susan are going to make significant gifts to Sally, it is important for Sally to have a will because her property would otherwise revert to her parents if she happened to die before they do. Her will could leave her property in trust for the benefit of her brother and her brother's family, assuming she stays single and has no children. Otherwise, she'd want to leave her property in trust for the benefit of her own children.

Eric should have a will which leaves his property to a trust for the benefit of his wife and children. If it happens that none of them outlives him, his property could pass to Sally.

What choices should the Huntingtons' make regarding executors?

Both Dick and Susan are bright and able people. For each to appoint the other as executor/executrix is a perfectly good choice. As an alternative, they can appoint a professional, either as sole executor or as co-executor with Dick or Susan.

What's really important is that if Dick or Susan serve, they must be sure to get professional help from either a bank trust officer or a lawyer, or both. Also, they must name an alternate executor to administer both estates in case they die at the same time. That alternate executor might be a bank, an attorney, or a trusted family member or friend. Again, a lay person should have professional assistance.

Estate Taxation

What should I know about estate taxes?

There are both state and federal estate taxes. The laws of different states vary: they may have an inheritance tax, an estate tax, or what is known as a sponge tax.

Many state estate taxes operate in line with the federal system; however, others will exclude or include different or additional property items when compared with the federal estate tax. No matter what the system, all estate taxes impose a tax on the estate itself, and the property which is distributed from the estate.

Inheritance taxes, on the other hand, are not imposed on the estate, but are assessed to the beneficiaries who actually receive the property.

A sponge tax is based on the federal credit for state death taxes. When computing the federal estate tax, a maximum credit for state death taxes will be allowed. A state which imposes a sponge tax will then collect as tax the amount of that credit.

After adjustments for all credits, the federal estate-tax rate for 1988 begins at approximately 37% and increases to 50%.

State tax rates vary considerably. In some instances they are higher than the federal tax as a result of credits allowed to the federal tax.

How does an estate plan minimize estate taxes?

First we compute the estate taxes which would be due if Dick died now, survived by Susan, without changing any asset ownership. Then we assume the reverse and determine the tax cost if Susan should die, survived by Dick. Finally we calculate the tax liability if both Dick and Susan should die, one soon after the other as a result of a disaster (such as a travel accident, for instance).

The results of these computations will tell us where the Huntingtons stand. Transferring assets between Dick and Susan, or into various tax-sheltering trusts, and gifting assets to other family members, are ways to help reduce potential estate-tax liabilities.

What's the estimate for estate taxes if Dick dies before Susan?

Generally, assuming that all of Dick's property passes to Susan, there would be no federal estate tax because all of the property would qualify for the marital deduction. That's true for any estate regardless of how large it is.

However, the estate may be taxed if Dick's retirement plan is deemed by the IRS to have an "excessive accumulation." This tax can be as much as 15% of the amount of excessive accumulation.

What if Susan dies first?

If Susan dies first and leaves everything to Dick, there will also be no federal estate-tax liability, because of the marital deduction, aside from the excise tax on pension benefits.

What happens if both Dick and Susan die?

We have to look at what happens to the second person's estate. Assume Dick dies and all of his property passes to Susan, and then she dies. There would be no tax on Dick's estate because all of his property passed to Susan and therefore qualified for the marital deduction. At that point, all of their assets would be owned by Susan.

The value of all of the Huntington's present assets is about $1.4 million. The tax computation is roughly as follows: $1.4 million less $70,000 representing 5% for estate administration expenses leaves $1.33 million. The federal estate tax on that amount in 1987 would be about $483,000.

From this amount we would subtract the unified credit, which allows a certain amount of that property to pass free of taxation. The unified credit is $192,800. In addition, the IRS allows a credit for state death taxes.

The credit is not the same amount as the taxes actually paid to the state, but is based on a table in the Internal Revenue Code. In Dick's case, a state death-tax credit of $53,520 will be allowed.

The tax to be paid nine months after the date of Susan's death would be approximately $236,680 ($483,000 minus $192,800 minus $53,520).

What can be done to help eliminate some of the estate-tax burden in this case?

First is to use an irrevocable life-insurance trust to remove $250,000 of life-insurance proceeds from Dick and Susan's estates. Second is to have Dick's property pass into a grantor trust.

On Dick's death part of the assets of his grantor trust will be held for Susan's benefit for her lifetime. Those assets will not be included in her estate when she dies because she is not given control of the property, only a lifetime interest. The amount of property which can be excluded from her estate in this way is $600,000.

The use of these two trusts could effectively remove from taxation in Susan's estate $850,000 (the $250,000 in life-insurance proceeds and $600,000 of property in Dick's grantor trust) .

Where does that leave the estate tax?

After these transactions, Susan's estate would be about $480,000 (less than the credit equivalent of $600,000) so the tax savings would be somewhere between $200,000 and $250,000. And that's not all. Additional property could be removed from taxation if Dick and Susan make gifts to their children and grandchildren.

Would Susan's estate plan do the same thing as Dick's?

Susan's grantor trust will have similar provisions so that if she dies before Dick, her trust would shelter the maximum amount of property from passing to Dick, to keep that property from being taxed in Dick's estate. Susan's trust would be a mirror-image of Dick's trust in that respect.

Trusts

What trust safeguards should the Huningtons undertake?

They could create a revocable living trust, called a "grantor" trust. Dick would create one for himself and Susan would create one for herself. If one of them were disabled, the assets of that person could be transferred into the trust and managed by the trustees for the benefit of the disabled person, as well as other family members.

Another good reason Dick or Susan might choose to create a grantor trust is to be relieved of management responsibilities. But generally, when a person transfers assets into a trust for his benefit during his lifetime, he will be the trustee at first, and successor trustees become active only if the person creating the trust is unable to act as trustee, or asks a successor to step in.

In addition, a grantor trust creates a sense of privacy. Since the records of the probate court are open to public scrutiny, a decedent's will is available for inspection at any time. However, a document creating a grantor trust will not be filed at the probate court, and thus escapes the public eye.

Does a grantor trust help provide for either Dick or Susan as survivor if one of them should die?

Yes. For example, if Dick were to die, his grantor trust would hold some of his property for the benefit of Susan. The trustees would manage the property so that Susan's available cash and financial management responsibilities would continue as before, with few changes.

Should their trusts be named as beneficiaries of their life-insurance policies?

Yes. If Dick owns his life-insurance policy and he has a grantor trust, the grantor trust should be named as the beneficiary. On the other hand, if Dick creates an irrevocable insurance trust, that trust should be both owner and beneficiary. In both instances, the purpose is to minimize taxation and preserve continuity of management for the insurance proceeds.

The trustees of Susan's grantor/living trust should also be the beneficiary of her insurance, for the same reasons. To complete the picture, the beneficiary of insurance on Eric's life should be the trustees of Eric's irrevocable life-insurance trust. Those trustees would hold the proceeds according to the terms of the trust.

141

Is there any significant difference between an irrevocable insurance trust and a grantor trust in how the trustees manage the life-insurance proceeds?

No. In either case, upon Dick's death the trustees would collect the life-insurance proceeds, and use those funds to provide for Susan and her children for the rest of her life. Then, at the time of her death, the remaining assets of the trust would pass to their children and grandchildren.

The difference is that if certain conditions are met, insurance proceeds received by the trustees of an irrevocable insurance trust will not be included in Dick's estate for estate tax purposes.

How would the Huntington's wills tie in with the trusts recommended?

Wills are definitely an important tool to insure that property gets to the right place with the minimum amount of disruption. The wills for Susan and Dick should be "pour-over wills," so-called because the wills are said to "pour" property into the decedent's trust.

Dick's will would provide first that his tangible personal property pass to Susan if she is living (otherwise to the children), and that the rest of his property pass to his revocable grantor trust.

In this way, Dick's property gets into his revocable trust, and has continuity of management. The assets would be controlled for the benefit of Susan and their family. Susan's will would do the same.

Who should Dick and Susan name as trustee for the various trusts?

With regard to the revocable living grantor trusts, Dick will act as his own trustee and Susan will act as her own trustee. They should provide for standby trustees to serve if either one of them is unavailable. For this, they each should have co-trustees, a bank trust officer, an attorney, or other independent person as one trustee, and a family member as the other. Sally might be a good choice.

What is the virtue of having a family member and an independent trustee as co-trustees?

The family member provides personal input to the professional trustee. The independent professional trustee separates the beneficiaries from control of the property, so that the trust will operate as an estate-tax shelter.

If the beneficiaries of a trust are also the trustees, and there is no independent or disinterested trustee involved, those beneficiaries may be considered to control the property for their own use. As a result, when the beneficiary dies, the value of the trust assets may be included in the beneficiary's estate. That would defeat the estate-tax sheltering benefit of the trusts.

Who should be trustees of the other trusts?

The second type of trust is an irrevocable trust to own the life-insurance policies and collect the proceeds. Independent trustees should be named. Perhaps a bank trust officer and an attorney or trusted family friend could serve as co-trustees.

The third kind of trust is a family trust for property transferred for the benefit of Sally and Eric and their children. This is the trust that would hold the vacation real estate. A family member and an independent trustee could serve as co-trustees.

Should a minor's trust be created for the benefit of Eric's children?

Yes, if there are going to be gifts for their benefit. The buzzword for this is a 2503C trust, after a section in the Internal Revenue Code. An independent trustee should serve under this trust.

Should the Huntingtons do anything beyond setting up the trusts?

Yes. It would be useful for them to put enough assets into these trusts to see them operate, and have an opportunity to get used to the procedures. Then, if anything happened to either Dick or Susan, the other one would already feel comfortable with the operation of the trust.

Lastly, it's important that the trust documents be drafted to provide for maximum flexibility by providing "spray" powers wherever appropriate, that is, give the trustees the power to distribute income and principal among a large number of beneficiaries. This way the trustees will have discretion to make the types of decisions that Dick or Susan would have made distributing their property.

Gifts

How do gifts fit into the Huntington's estate planning?

A recommended gift program for the Huntingtons would include gifts to their daughter Sally, the surgeon. She seems responsible, and current gift tax laws would allow Susan and Dick each to give $10,000 a year to Sally without incurring any gift tax.

In the same way, Dick and Susan could give $20,000 a year to Eric, and the same amount to each of Eric's three children, and his wife, if they wish.

Wait a minute, that's $120,000 a year! Are Dick and Susan really going to want to do that?

Perhaps not that much, or not every year. But the point is that they can transfer $120,000 a year to their family if they wish, free of taxation.

Of course, as described, Eric and his family would be getting a lot more each year than Sally, so the Huntingtons might want to consider ways of equalizing the shares at some point.

How can they equalize gift shares?

One way is to use part of Susan's and part of Dick's unified credit each year to augment the $10,000 annual gift-tax exclusion. The unified credit allows an individual to transfer property in value up to $600,000 without paying gift or estate tax.

Thus, Sally, Eric and Eric's family could receive equal gifts each year. Once a person utilizes a portion of the credit during his/her lifetime, however, that portion is not available at death.

Is it wise for the Huntingtons to transfer property outright to Eric, his wife, or his young children?

The Huntingtons would probably not object to transferring $10,000 to Eric or his wife, but they may have problems with such a gift to the children. Dick could create a trust for the benefit of one or all of Eric's children; however, the trust must contain certain provisions to insure that the transfer constitutes a valid gift.

The trust must provide that each child will have the right to make an annual withdrawal from the trust. This is a "Crummey Power," named after a tax case in which this arrangement was approved as a valid gifting technique.

However, if the trust is for the benefit of all of Eric's children and each child is given the right to withdraw $10,000, but fails to do so, it is said that the right of withdrawal has lapsed. Certain technical precautions should be taken to avoid adverse estate or gift tax consequences.

Are there other methods for transferring property to minors?

Yes. Some states have laws known as the Uniform Gifts to Minors Act (UGMA) or Uniform Transfer to Minors Act (UTMA). They are simple arrangements by which a donor can transfer property to a minor; ownership of the property goes to the minor at age eighteen (UGMA) or twenty-one (UTMA).

Is there any way Dick and Susan can take the summer house out of their estates, yet continue to use it?

Yes. Dick could create a trust for the benefit of his children and his grandchildren. Every year he and Susan could transfer an undivided fractional interest in the property to the trust. The fractional interest would not exceed the tax-free combined gift allowance of $20,000 per person per year.

For instance, if the summer home is worth $200,000, a one-tenth undivided interest would be worth $20,000. In the first year Dick and Susan could give an undivided two-tenths interest to the trust. By the use of Crummey powers, $20,000 worth of the gift could apply to Sally and $20,000 to Eric. Therefore, there would be no gift taxes.

When using this type of gifting program, however, precautionary attention should be paid to the lapse of the Crummey power. Dick and Susan would also have to put enough cash in the trust to pay the expenses of the upkeep of the property.

There are some other details which Dick and Susan would have to attend to so that the value of the property will not be brought back into their estates.

What sort of details?

They have to do with reducing the amount of control and beneficial interest Dick and Susan have over and in the property once it has been given to the trust.

The general rule is that even though an individual places property in a trust, if he or she retains a certain amount of control over or beneficial interest in the property, the value will be brought back into the estate.

An individual must decide which elements of control he wishes to retain or give up, and balance that with the possibility that the value will not escape estate taxation. For example, we might suggest that Dick and Susan sign a lease for their use of the value of the property given the children.

Are there any differences between gifting to children and gifting to grandchildren?

Yes. Although it is permissible to give each of your grandchildren $10,000 or (in the case of a consenting spouse) $20,000 annually without a gift tax, the current version of the generation-skipping transfer tax must be considered for estates over $1 million.

What about the old version?

A generation-skipping tax has been around for about ten years, but it was repealed retroactively, and anyone who paid a tax under that law is entitled to a refund. Executors and trustees of estates who have paid the tax should file a claim for a refund with the IRS.

How does the current generation-skipping tax operate?

The tax is imposed at the rate of 55% in 1987 and 50% in 1988 and future years, and applies to all transfers where estate and gift taxes are avoided by causing property to "skip over" a generation below that of the transferor.

For example, if a grandfather decided to give $100,000 directly to his grandchild, this would be a "direct skip." The IRS would not have taxed it in his child's estate; therefore, it is taxed when it passes to the grandchild.

Would the value of property placed in a trust escape the generation-skipping tax?

No. In addition to being imposed on direct skips, it is also imposed on taxable terminations and taxable distributions under trusts.

A "taxable termination" occurs when a trust ceases to exist and the assets are distributed to an individual at least two generations below the grantor. A "taxable distribution" occurs when a trust makes a distribution to a grandchild or great grandchild.

If Susan is the last one to die and she leaves her property to her grandchildren, will her estate will pay both an estate tax and a generation-skipping transfer tax?

That's the intent of the law, but there are some exceptions and exemptions which will provide relief for the Huntingtons. Any individual whose estate is $1 million or less does not have to worry about this tax. A person is entitled to transfer up to $1 million during his lifetime or at his death.

Also, if a transfer vests before January 1, 1990, it is possible to transfer up to $2 million to each grandchild without the imposition of the tax. Additionally, any transfer for education or health care is exempt.

Finally, if Eric dies before Susan, his children move up a generation and the tax is not imposed on transfers to them, but would be on transfers to great grandchildren.

Will all of these trusts and gifts make Dick and Susan feel that they are in a financial straight jacket?

Their overall financial plan would make sure they have sufficient assets and income for their own needs before entering into any gifting program or executing an irrevocable trust. They would have the peace of mind of having trustees oversee the use of property for the benefit of Eric, Sally, and their grandchildren.

The plan would be extremely flexible, allowing Dick and Susan to pass property to their children and grandchildren and save significant expenses and taxes. It would also allow the Huntingtons to keep significant control over their property during their lifetime.

This concludes the Huntington family case study.

Index